Michael **Schumacher**

Michael
Schumacher

The Ferrari Years by *Christopher Hilton* ***Second edition***

First edition published in February 2000
Second edition published in April 2001

A catalogue record for this book is
available from the British Library

ISBN 1 85960 829 9

Library of Congress catalog card no 00-136551

Haynes North America Inc.,
861 Lawrence Drive, Newbury Park,
California 91320, USA

Published by Haynes Publishing, Sparkford, Nr Yeovil, Somerset BA22 7JJ, UK.
Tel: 01963 442030 Fax: 01963 440001
Int.tel: +44 1963 442030 Fax: +44 1963 440001
E-mail: sales@haynes-manuals.co.uk
Web site: www.haynes.co.uk

Previous page: Leap of joy. Suzuka, 2000. (Formula One Pictures)

Designed and typeset by G&M, Raunds, Northamptonshire
Printed and bound in Great Britain by J.H. Haynes & Co. Ltd., Sparkford

Contents

Introduction and acknowledgements

This is a book about one man expressing himself at the very top of his chosen medium and bearing the highest expectations every time he tried. At one level it can be simply told. Michael Schumacher was being paid $30m a year – more than any other racing driver, ever – to bring Ferrari the World Championship for the first time since 1979.

At another level – the intersection where Formula 1's ferocity and awesome technology meet – it is daunting in all its complexities. That's why I am particularly indebted to senior Ferrari personnel for confiding their views from the inside. Ross Brawn, the Technical Director, showed great courtesy as well as candour; Rory Byrne, who designs the cars, and Nigel Stepney, who makes sure they run, were both extremely helpful in a touching way. John Barnard (now of B3 Technologies) used to design the cars and was mercilessly honest about Schumacher, and himself.

There's a third dimension too. Schumacher has completed four seasons with Ferrari, and at the core of that period remain the races: the chosen medium. Some are the most astonishing and profound ever created by a racing driver. Some are bitter, angry things, violent in their physics and their emotions; some are triumphant, and a very few plain ordinary. But all are here; and so is how Schumacher rationalised what he was doing at them.

Curiously, although Schumacher hasn't yet brought Ferrari the Drivers' championship they yearn for, the perception of his skills has kept on increasing. The races show why.

Many others helped with this book (some inadvertently) and so thanks to the ITV team, London: Martin Brundle, Louise Goodman and James Allen. I pay tribute to German television Channel RTL.

Thanks to Pino Allievi of *La Gazzetta dello Sport;* Alan Burgess of *Karting* magazine; Owen O'Mahoney; Thomas Muchow of the Steinheide Kartbahn, Kerpen-Manheim; Lindsay Morle of Williams Grand Prix Engineering; Inge and Barbel for the usual instant and painstaking translations; Claudia Berro and the Ferrari Press Office for their invaluable service; Rosetta Izzo for her efficiency; Giancarlo Fisichella and Julia Horden of Benetton Formula Ltd; Brian Hart; Jean-Carl Berger of TAG-Heuer sent me many, many laps times; E.L. Gordon; Alexander Wurz, Johnny Herbert; Matt Bishop, Group Editor of Haymarket Publications for the background to a fascinating interview of Schumacher by Damon Hill, which first appeared in *F1 Racing* magazine; Viktoria Tischer for translation; Roger Chapman.

Straight from the grid

'I am not a movie star. Either things come naturally to you or they don't. You cannot learn emotions.' Michael Schumacher was speaking in Italian, which itself was a news item, that day as the 2001 season beckoned. He and the Italian public were growing towards each other, and had been since before he won the World Championship for himself and for them. Now he was reaching towards beautiful phrases in their own language, rather than in English, to touch *their* emotions.

Two ends and a beginning, each played out to a different mood. The ends were in Japan in 1999 and 2000, the first bringing rancour amidst a moral maze, the second bestowing upon him and Ferrari the first drivers' World Championship in a couple of generations. The beginning was in Italy and compressed itself onto how he would win the title again.

Maranello, 29 January 2001. The Ferrari heartland was a place of passion. As Schumacher arrived for the launch of the new car, several hundred supporters chanted 'champions, champions,' and they might have been speaking for the whole of Italy. He insisted that his motivation (the favourite Formula 1 word) remained undiluted. 'I am a natural,' he would say. 'I want to be at the limit and there is still a lot of joy for me in driving.

I can't say I am more motivated because that is impossible, but the weight is off our shoulders and the motivation now is to improve constantly.' He looked in a powerful mood, crisp and concentrated. He had good reason.

Suzuka, 5–8 October 2000. Going in, the weight was still on their shoulders, oppressive and inescapable, as it had been every season since Jody Scheckter became Ferrari's last World Champion in 1979.

Schumacher came to the sixteenth round of the 2000 championship with an eight-point lead over Mika Hakkinen. Schumacher and David Coulthard, Hakkinen's team-mate at McLaren, had rubbed wheels when Schumacher muscled through in the United States Grand Prix, the round before Suzuka. 'Immediately after, I was angry,' Schumacher would say, because Coulthard appeared to move over on him. However, 'after seeing the television pictures I had to change my opinion.' That apology cleared the debris of the season away – Schumacher and Coulthard had been squabbling for months. Suzuka, with half the planet watching, could now be a clean fight.

The Formula 1 community gathered, as it does, on the Thursday. In the concrete grandstand opposite the pits thousands of

Japanese sat in silence. They would see, this day, no car going round. They wanted a glimpse of a driver, a feeling of proximity but, out of their sight, Schumacher and Hakkinen shook hands then faced the Media. The two men have a mutual respect which is genuine and, the Hakkinen camp tell me discreetly, not something they talk about in public.

Question to Hakkinen: will you be doing anything different? 'No. Nothing really. Just that I will be braking a couple of metres later for every corner.'

Schumacher: 'I'll have to brake five metres later, I guess.'

Hakkinen: 'But then you'll be in the gravel.'

Schumacher: 'We'll be together ...' [LAUGHTER]

Coulthard applied some cleansing of his own. 'I have a lot of respect for Michael. He has earned that because he is hard, aggressive and hungry in every condition, wet or dry. There are, however, enough indications that when Michael is desperate he is prepared to do something that people are likely to question as unsporting. He should push it to the limit but not beyond. I will do what I can to help the team, but I will do so within the rules and they would not ask me to go beyond that.'

There was an earthquake in Japan on the Friday. Its epicentre was some 150 kilometres away and measured 7.1 on the Richter Scale, reducing to 3.9 when it reached Suzuka at 1.30 but still strong enough to shake the pits and offices for 30 seconds and make people run outside. Schumacher was driving but 'out on the track I did not feel a thing'. He finished this practice 0.611 seconds faster than Hakkinen.

The second practice was tighter, Hakkinen 0.139 seconds up but, the sense of theatre mounting, everything concentrated onto Saturday's qualifying. This, too, Schumacher felt would be very tight. Winter sunlight fell across his face, the peak of his cap casting a shadow across his eyes, as he said 'we feel optimistic because we know that we have a very good car and if we get the maximum out of this car we

know we can do it but then that's the point: do we always get the maximum or not? And what about the other side?'

He strode purposefully to his pit with his overall top folded down over his waist revealing the white tee-shirt underneath. His face looked sombre, preoccupied. He vanished into the bosom of the pit still striding. The sun was weaker now, fashioning a narrow wedge of shadow from the pit lane wall. Within the bosom he sat, hands clasped, and made a joke to a team member. He held the smile and seemed in no hurry. 'In my view, the circuit wasn't in good condition in the early stage [of the session]. There was no point in going out early and just wasting a set of tyres.' He and Ross Brawn, the Technical Director, began to concentrate on what would happen later.

Of the front runners, Coulthard was out first – the sun dipped behind cloud – and did 1m 36.633s. Some 25 minutes in, Schumacher emerged, pulling his visor down, twisting the car rightwards down the pit lane. He seemed to strike the visor with his forearm, flipping it up. He pulled it down again. As he circled towards the hot lap Hakkinen emerged. Schumacher attacked: smooth in all his sharpness and very near the limit. As he was going faster than Coulthard had in the third sector, Hakkinen was going faster than he had in the first sector. Schumacher crossed the line at *1:36.094* and Hakkinen at *1:36.168*.

Schumacher quickest by 0.074.

With 21 minutes to go Hakkinen was out, in the second sector went *0.098* faster and crossed the line at *1:36.017*.

Hakkinen quickest by 0.077.

Schumacher came out with 17 minutes to go, soothed the Ferrari round, built towards the lap and attacked again. The car looked sensuous now, a beautiful, predatory animal. He crossed the line at *1:35.908*.

Schumacher quickest by 0.109.

Hakkinen, in the cockpit in the McLaren pit, gazed at a television monitor and briefly shook his head. Eleven minutes to go and he made his response, Schumacher now watching the monitor.

Hakkinen was slower by *0.043* in the first sector – Schumacher's expression didn't react to that – and slower by *0.025* in the second sector. But not the third. He crossed the line at *1:35.834*.

Hakkinen quickest by 0.074.

Schumacher smiled, fleeting, wistful; and he responded. Brawn had chosen this moment with exquisite timing – a minimum of traffic. Three and a half minutes to go and Schumacher forced the Ferrari through the sweepers beyond turn one, forced it through the first sector but was *0.039* slower. In the second sector he rattled the kerbs, the sun drawing shadows from the wheels, and he went *0.012* quicker. As he moved into the third sector Hakkinen emerged in a flurry of movement. Schumacher crossed the line at *1:35.825*.

Schumacher quickest by 0.009.

Hakkinen began his final lap. Schumacher saw 'the first two sectors, then I was a little more quiet' – Hakkinen *0.002* up in the first, *0.088* down in the second. 'I knew it could have been a tight qualifying situation [now] and if he had got the lap together either of us could have been on pole.' Hakkinen crossed the line at *1:36.018*. Schumacher had pole by that *0.009* – centimetres hewn from Suzuka's 5.8 kilometres. The Ferrari pit surrendered to broad-grinning and back-slapping. Schumacher drank from a bottle, examined the times on a monitor, strode up the pit lane and – as Hakkinen's McLaren was being pushed into the *parc fermé* garage – stopped. He gazed intently at it, dissecting it.

He went to the Press Conference and someone said 'you seem much quieter, and more reflective on getting the job done here this weekend than you usually are. How much pressure are you under?'

In defence of the world – Schumacher at the launch of the 2001 Ferrari. (Formula One Pictures)

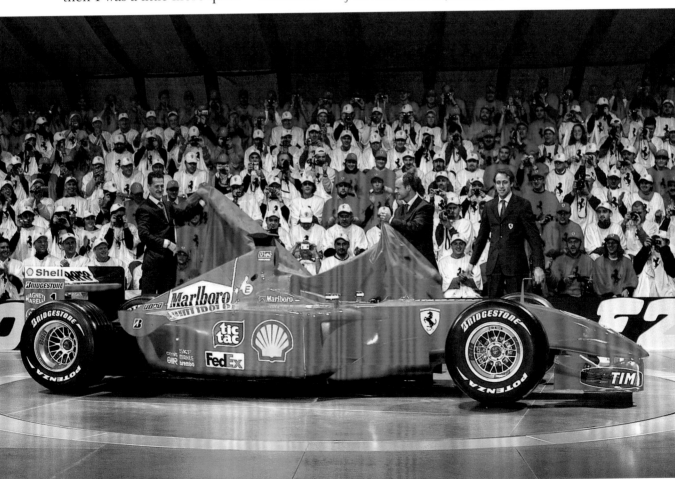

He dissected that. 'Naturally this is not a race like any other. We can finish the Championship here, but there is no point in celebrating this pole position big time. It's nice, but it isn't the end result. We will have to fight for that very hard tomorrow. We are ready.'

The 30-minute Sunday morning warm-up is a curious creature, given almost no publicity but arguably of more significance than qualifying because here cars run in race trim. Qualifying's reticence, where a session can be ten minutes old before you see a car, is reversed by an immediate cavalcade; and there was one here, Schumacher among it. Under a leaden sky, he did a 1:38.005 – Hakkinen 1:38.526 – and that was a real gap.

The weather forecast suggested rain during the race.

I'm thanking you now because in an hour I'll be drunk

Half a world away, back in Maranello, it rained in the darkness and the Ferrari faithful sheltered under umbrellas as they prepared to watch the race on a giant screen. Ferrari flags fluttered, saddened in the rain but defiant too. Young men jumped up and down in front of a television camera while others staged a mock funeral, carrying a coffin with Mercedes (whose engines McLaren had) on it to a local church and then the Ferrari headquarters. In Schumacher's home town of Kerpen some three thousand people prepared to watch, most of them wearing blood-red clothing and waving Ferrari flags confidently. Young men jumped up and down in front of a television camera. A communion held both communities.

Luca di Montezemolo, Ferrari's President, telephoned Schumacher. He 'listened to Schumi, then I only said *I thank you. I am doing it now because in an hour's time I will be drunk*' – inebriated with delight.

At Suzuka the cars came to the grid. A young Japanese lady in a kimono stood by Schumacher's bay holding a placard on a pole. Schumacher nosed the Ferrari into the bay and the team surrounded it. He got out and surveyed the car, chatted to Brawn: slightly bearded, bespectacled, his earphones with their antennae resembling a Viking helmet. The mood was calm, *anglo-saxon*. Schumacher gazed at the sky searching for signs of the rain, gave a brief TV interview – if this side of the track or that bestowed an initial advantage – and chatted to Brawn again.

The grid cleared like a sudden migration, leaving the twin column of cars alone. They covered the formation lap, Schumacher taking them round at a respectable pace. They settled on the grid facing 53 laps. Hakkinen was away fast, Schumacher slewing full across towards him – wheelspin, he'd explain. Hakkinen veered clear but didn't back off and, into turn one, led. 'Mika was very quick and there was nothing I could do.' The race might have been settled already. They drew away from the others and waltzed lap after lap, the gap expanding to 2.5 seconds, contracting to less than 1.0; waltzed to the first pit stops. Hakkinen made his on lap 22: stationary 6.8 seconds, taking on fuel for 13 laps. Already Brawn was bringing Schumacher in next lap: stationary 7.4 seconds, fuel for 15 laps. When Hakkinen made his second stop Schumacher would have those two laps to do what he'd always done, create.

At lap 30 drizzle fell from a dark sky and wind raked the circuit but they waltzed on, the gap expanding and contracting again until, in this drizzle, Schumacher closed up. Then, into the chicane Ricardo Zonta (BAR) let Hakkinen through but almost brushed against Schumacher's rear wheel. Nightmare: if Zonta had been centimetres further over the history of motor racing might have been altered forever.

On lap 37 Hakkinen did stop again (stationary 7.4 seconds) and Schumacher had the two laps for the creation. He had to gain enough time to pit himself and hold the lead – 'this was the crucial time' – but both Jaguars lay in front of him. Eddie Irvine, in one of them, scampered clear but Schumacher didn't pass Johnny

Herbert in the other until they began the next lap. 'The traffic cost me a little bit of time.' Rain fell, Brawn on the pit lane scanning it. As Schumacher flowed out of the chicane on his 'in' lap Alexander Wurz (Benetton) spun but there was just enough room to get through. Nightmare: 'it was moving backwards in front of me and I didn't know where he was going to go'.

Schumacher pitted. 'I didn't think I had done enough. It was spitting with rain and I thought I hadn't gone as fast as I should have done.' Wrong. He'd gained half a second – the creation – and was stationary for only 6.0 seconds. While Schumacher travelled with agonising slowness down the pit lane, a prisoner of the speed limit, Brawn watched for Hakkinen to come from the chicane and seize the lead.

'It's looking good,' Brawn said on the radio. Schumacher wasn't sure about that.

'It's looking good,' Brawn updated in a running commentary. Still Schumacher wasn't sure about that.

'It's looking good,' Brawn continued.

Schumacher waited to hear the fateful words *sorry, it's not looking good enough.* With the pit lane wall between him and the track, he could see absolutely nothing of where Hakkinen was.

'It's looking bloody good!' Brawn said.

Schumacher would remember this as an amazing moment and, as he regained the track, Hakkinen was far, far back in the distance. Twelve laps remained, history beckoning. Schumacher 'just hoped nothing broke' on the car, survived a wobble in the wet, withstood late Hakkinen pressure and Ferrari dreams came true.

When he had brought the car to rest he sat for a long moment with his head bowed in supplication before the fact: a private moment. Behind barriers a gaggle of Ferrari team-members in their blood-red uniforms had abandoned themselves: their faces were consumed. Some cried, some clapped wildly, some waved their arms, some brandished clenched fists. Some looked suddenly exhausted in their exultancy as if, after so long, the moment was too much.

Jean Todt, the small, almost birdlike Frenchman running the Ferrari team, had dipped into the cockpit and clasped Schumacher's gloved hands. Irvine, who'd helped him towards this at Ferrari and left before the consummation, stretched down and shook the gloved hands. Todt patted the side of Irvine's forehead – affection – and then Irvine melted away. Schumacher removed the steering wheel and pumped a fist. Todt, meticulous, set the steering wheel lightly down on the nosecone and he melted away.

Schumacher was alone. He levered himself up in the cockpit, raised his head, clenched both fists and worked them to and fro like pistons. He clasped the helmet and bowed his head in supplication again. He was

When he got out of the Ferrari he walked like a free man

shedding the weight and when he got out of the car he walked like a free man. The rest was lost in the pull and push of emotion: his wife Corinna weeping with joy, everyone embracing everyone, two Ferrari mechanics shaving their heads. Schumacher conducted the Italian national anthem on the rostrum, Todt was so soaked in champagne he tried to wring it from his shirt, Brawn explained that, unemotional by nature, he was trying to control his emotions, and Hakkinen was utterly gracious in defeat.

In Maranello, Father Alberto Bernardoni apologised for not ringing the bells as Schumacher crossed the line. He'd been saying Mass at that moment.

Di Montezemolo said: 'It is the first victory since the passing away of the Company's founder, Enzo Ferrari, in 1988 and Gianni Agnelli of the Fiat dynasty [who own Ferrari] said his first thought was how happy the old boy would be today.'

Italy's President, Carlo Azeglio Ciampi, said: 'Finally after 21 years we earned it.' Gerhard Schroder, the Bundeskanzler, sent a message of congratulations which arrived so swiftly it surprised Schumacher as well touching him.

The celebrations at the track that night had to be improvised because Schumacher insisted nothing be planned in advance 'as I felt it would be unlucky'. Heavy rain was falling but that didn't matter. The party really did begin. It was, we are assured, of historical proportions.

It had all been very different the year before.

Suzuka, *28–31 October 1999.* All weekend he'd worn his different faces. On the Thursday it was the boy next door, relaxed and a little naughty. He made his way to the Media Centre for a set-piece press conference and there espied Martin Brundle, his team-mate at Benetton in 1992 and now a television commentator. Schumacher came over and feigned tweaking Brundle's ear before they fell to affectionate banter spiced with occasional naughtiness. Schumacher wielded his broad, warm smile and at such moments he can look something more than the boy next door. He becomes the most ordinary bloke in the world. He wore blue jeans and sneakers. Corinna, in casual slacks and jumper, was outside the Ferrari office chatting and looking exactly like the girl next door.

He handled the press conference effortlessly and gave a secondary conference in German. He was hemmed so tightly he vanished within the journalists. Microphones and tape recorders were pressed virtually into his mouth but he talked quite naturally. Cameramen held their cameras over the heads of the journalists and the flash bulbs went off like explosions of lightning. They did not make him blink once.

Towards the end he was enjoying himself, making jokes and creating laughter although – inevitably – one serious topic could not be avoided. Would he, on the Sunday, help team-mate Irvine to the championship? The topic had become hot

Looking into heaven: Schumacher wins the 2000 World Championship and, just for this instant, isn't smiling. The weight of history made Mika Hakkinen and David Coulthard seem sombre, too. (Schlegelmilch)

JAPANESE GRAND PRIX 2000
SUZUKA

in mid-season, when Schumacher crashed at Silverstone leaving his own championship hopes destroyed. At the Malaysian Grand Prix two weeks before Suzuka he had returned from his injuries and masterfully, majestically manipulated the whole race so that Irvine won. Would he now help Irvine to the great prize? His prize. He seemed ambivalent: 'I have said right from the start that I won't have to be a support to Eddie, but I will have to win the race to ensure the Constructors' Championship [for Ferrari], and in doing that I will be helping Eddie as much as possible.' To take the title Hakkinen needed to win the race and if he didn't, fourth place would suffice for Irvine. So if Schumacher came first Hakkinen might well be in trouble.

On the Friday the face was that of a racer again as he moved to third fastest in the practice session behind Hakkinen and Coulthard. Then at 4.20 he went to the office of the FIA, the sport's governing body: Room 208 on the top floor. Schumacher prepared to be interviewed by Damon Hill for *F1 Racing* magazine. It had been arranged by Matt Bishop, Group Editor of Haymarket Motorsport Magazines because Hill was to guest-edit *F1 Racing* for one issue after his retirement.

Bishop had been astonished to learn that apart from obligatory politeness the longest conversation Hill and Schumacher had had was after the birth of Schumacher's first child. Hill went up to him, shook his hand and said 'you're a dad now same as me'.

Schumacher: 'Yes, yes, that's right.'

Hill: 'How's the baby, how's your wife?'

Schumacher: 'Fine, fine.'

However, Bishop adds: 'I believe Damon was one of only three drivers to visit Schumacher in hospital after the accident at Silverstone. His brother Ralf and Jean Alesi were the other two.'

A great deal of what Schumacher had

to say carried authentic insights and although I'm only quoting a small portion (with kind permission) the extracts are striking.

Schumacher's confidence was, Hill said, 'very apparent from the outside' to which he replied 'I don't have the kind of confidence you think I might have. Not at all. Actually, I question myself very often. When things don't go well, I always question myself first. And I try very hard – I will never give up trying. So, you know, personally I don't believe I have as much

The man with the ultimate power – Schumacher wins the 2000 Japanese Grand Prix and, at last, his third world title. (Schlegelmilch)

self-belief as people think from the outside. But then in relation to my competitors, I don't know. I don't know what their level of self-belief is. I can't say that.'

Hill mentioned that Schumacher had shown emotion on the podium: 'You'd jump up, stick your fist in the air – even if you were second.'

Schumacher: 'In my view I'm a very stable person. I don't have many ups and downs. That's why my emotions are not often seen as dramatic, certainly not as dramatic as maybe people want to see.

And it really takes a lot to make that happen. You have seen me very often – like you say, it's my trademark – being excited. You have seen me very rarely being depressed and showing those kind of other emotions.' And he made the comparison again then, as he would at Maranello in 2001: 'I don't need the kind of thing you see with some pop stars or movie stars, you know, extremes of emotion.'

On the Saturday the face was as we had known it, greyhound-lean and utterly

concentrated. He summoned a stunning lap of 1:37.470 which was not to be beaten. Afterwards, pressed about the Irvine situation (Irvine had qualified fifth), he said: 'I don't think my tactics will change. It is very clear that the best thing which can happen for us is if I win the race. I will give the most help I can for Eddie and the team. That will be the strategy.'

On the Sunday he put his different faces on again. Fifty minutes to go before the race and brother Ralf was chatting to someone behind the pits. Schumacher – ear plugs in, overalls hanging from his waist like a peeled banana – was moving past him and took a good-natured swipe above his head. Ralf turned, thought *it's only him*, turned back.

The start went wrong because Hakkinen was away fast, Schumacher slewing full across the track towards him. By then Hakkinen was clearly in the lead, the race decided. At no stage could Schumacher threaten him and it continued like that lap after lap in a sort of suspended animation. More than half way through the race Coulthard went off and destroyed the McLaren's nosecone. He pitted and emerged in front of Schumacher but a lap down. The rules insist that Coulthard was entitled to hold Schumacher up (and thus help Hakkinen) but on sight of waved blue flags had to get out of the way. Coulthard was in no particular hurry to do that, which made Schumacher very angry. Hakkinen won.

On the podium Schumacher wore his best smile. Then he, Hakkinen and Irvine trooped off to the televised question-and-answer session. In the McLaren pit the personnel watched on television monitors. The interviewer said to him *going through the race, you began to get quite close to Mika but you got held up by David Coulthard. You seemed very annoyed when you went past him.*

Schumacher's face moved to somewhere between stern and severe. 'Yes. I mean Mika is definitely a great champion today, he made the championship by winning the race so there is no reason why he shouldn't celebrate that 100% but the

team should wonder why they ask the drivers to do things like they have done – because it was a different thing in Malaysia when I was racing actually for position and not being lapped. You can play tactics. But if you are lapped ...'

(Ron Dennis, watching in the McLaren pit, said: 'Here it is, having a go at David.')

'... you should give space and David passed many blue flags. He had a kind of problem but he was really driving zig-zagging ...'

(A ripple of anger spread through the McLaren pit and someone shouted 'bullshit'.)

'... and actually I'm not sure whether I should believe whether Spa [they crashed in 1998] wasn't really done purposely, the way he behaved today, because I didn't expect him doing such a thing when it was clear he was out of the race, he was lapped. I am very disappointed seeing a manoeuvre from a guy which nobody expected to see – because I was really challenging Mika ... I think this situation cost me about ten seconds so I'm very disappointed.' Coulthard was angry too.

Into the evening Schumacher returned to being the boy next door. Around the pits he played out high-jinks and later, according to one press agency, 'some reports claimed the former World Champion was drunk'. Luca di Montezemolo dismissed this with delightful elegance. 'I would rather have a Schumacher who gets drunk sometimes and jokes and laughs. If he was too serious it would be a problem. It's fine as long as he only gets drunk once a year.'

Quietly, before he left Suzuka that evening in 1999, Schumacher said 'next year will be my time'. It is what people say, but we know now how right the prediction was. We know now how, returning to this same Suzuka in October 2000, he did more than restore ultimate dignity to Ferrari – he banished all doubt that he was one of the greatest racing drivers who has ever lived. How did it come about? Let's start at the very beginning, not Maranello in January 2001 but *the* beginning ...

chapter one

Come together

That Saturday in early January 1969 Chris Amon won the New Zealand Grand Prix at a place called Pukekohe, driving a Ferrari. The race was the start of the Tasman Series, and nothing to do with the World Championship. But entries were being announced for the opening round of the Formula 1 season, at Kyalami in South Africa on 1 March: two cars each from Lotus, McLaren, BRM, Brabham, Matra, and Ferrari. Evidently the latter caused mild surprise because, a short time before, Enzo Ferrari had announced he'd only be entering one car for most of the Championship. Now, without explanation, he had changed his mind. At this stage he nominated one driver, Amon.

Always it had been so, since Ferrari founded his team in Modena – an ancient Italian town mid-way along the old route between Milan and the Adriatic – on 16 November 1929 and its symbol, the Prancing Horse, became a national, then a global, icon. In 1943, with the hope of escaping Allied bombing, the company moved to Maranello, a town of some 10,000 inhabitants 16km from Modena.

Enzo Ferrari was by turns an autocrat with, when he wanted, the coarsened mannerisms and cunning of a peasant, a dictator who ruled by fear and intrigue, a womaniser on a scale which only Darwin's Theory of Evolution can explain, a patri-

cian who could seem becalmed and benign; and a genius. No other word will do. The racing cars he made were so desirable that damn near every driver wanted to drive them, the road cars so desirable that he could pick his customers.

On the Friday of that Pukekohe weekend a boy was born to Rolf and Elisabeth Schumacher. They were entirely ordinary people – Rolf was a builder, good with his hands – and the chances were that their son would be ordinary too. He'd grow up in Kerpen, a solid Rhineland town of industry, banking and a little agriculture within commuting distance of Cologne. Kerpen is built round an old church and modest in its pretensions, no tourist office or tourist maps even. Kerpen would shape him. The locals say you go to Aachen over by the Belgian border and they're boring, you go south to the Eifel Mountains and they're boring, but here we like to live, that's how we are and that's how he is.

Chris Amon was the latest in a dynasty drawn to Maranello to tame the Prancing Horse. He'd been trying since 1967. Others would follow, coming from several continents. All this is well known: a mystical team which fed its own mythology. It was, in every sense, a long way from the Rhineland.

Kerpen is the central axis of a hub of little linked communities. One, the other side of the Aachen-Cologne autobahn, is Horrem. It too is modern, busy, quietly prosperous. From here, in

The stairway to a big future ... traditional tight curves ... and mother nature returning. The now-abandoned kart track at Horrem where the whole thing began, and was this the paddock? (Author)

18

1957, went a man called Wolfgang von Trips to try the taming. He was an aristocrat, hugely popular, and might have been Germany's first World Champion; but he died in a Ferrari at Monza in 1961, and 13 spectators died too. Enzo Ferrari wrote an autobiography and entitled it 'My Terrible Joys'.

In 1969, as Rolf and Elisabeth took the baby home, Amon was partnered by a Mexican, Pedro Rodriguez. That season they managed just seven points between them. The Ferrari 312 with its V12 engine was not a success. A year later the neat Belgian Jacky Ickx might have won the title after the Championship leader – Jochen Rindt (Lotus) – was killed at Monza, but he didn't, and was glad not to rob a dead man of his due. Ickx's partner, the Swiss Clay Regazzoni, was third. Across the early 1970s Ferrari were descending, and in 1973 Ickx finished with only 12 points. His new partner, the Italian Arturo Merzario, had six.

In Kerpen, the Schumacher parents gave their four-year-old son a go-kart powered by a motorcycle engine. The boy would remember it well. His father 'loved to be messing about in the garage and one day he decided on a strange idea: to take my go-kart, a kids' go-kart which I wasn't using any more, and take an old motorcycle and put its engine in the kart. That's how it happened.' On this he puttered around the streets. Rolf told his son 'drive carefully and not too quickly' but mythology insists that Michael lost control on a corner and used a lamp-post to stop.

In 1974 Lauda came to Ferrari, Lauda of exalted Viennese extraction who'd remember being taken to Fiorano near Modena where Ferrari tested and 'suddenly I saw all the technical marvels: a private race track with automatic time-keeping, with closed circuit television and computers.' He saw 'a comparably vast team of fitters, engineers, administrators. I couldn't imagine how such a set-up could fail to win.' It was an exact distillation of what others before him had felt, and others after him would feel. Lauda

won the Championship in 1975.

In June that summer a brother was born, Ralf.

Lauda nearly died defending the Championship when his Ferrari crashed and became a fireball at the Nürburgring in 1976. Instead he became The Living Legend and won it again in 1977. Face for ever seared, Lauda deepened the Ferrari mystique.

Far into the future Lauda would refer to the kid from Kerpen as 'the talent of the century', but as yet young Michael was living, as he said, 'the childhood of any other boy, playing football, climbing trees, getting into a little trouble.'

Lauda left after a furious political row and a young Canadian, Gilles Villeneuve, replaced him. Villeneuve was intuitively audacious in a racing car but had a simple, direct honesty which disarmed everyone and Italy prepared to surrender to him,

although not quite yet because 1978 proved difficult: he was learning. His partner, the Argentine Carlos Reutemann, finished third.

Part of Horrem spreads up a hillside. Narrow streets follow this contour, side-streets to right and left. Along one, detached houses nestle in the bosom of respectable suburbia. At the end you climbed a curving path into woodland. Here a tiny kart track – a ribbon of tarmacadam – contorted between trees and clumps of bushes. Long grass grew. Michael was nine, and felt drawn to this place. He couldn't compete, of course: too young.

In 1979 an erudite and single-minded South African, Jody Scheckter, partnered

The move from Horrem to the bigger kart track at Kerpen-Manheim. Schumacher outside the cafeteria and, years later, where he loved to be – in amongst the karts. (Formula One Pictures)

Villeneuve. It made for a good balance, Villeneuve pouring uncalculated passion into every lap he covered, Scheckter calculating a route to the Championship, which he took at Monza. That late afternoon of 9 September was hot and dry. Scheckter rounded the Parabolica curve and accelerated along the wide start-finish straight, Villeneuve holding back to give him the moment. People spilled from the pits to witness it, brandishing fists in intoxication. A common impulse seized the whole of Monza. Thousands in the grandstands opposite the pits were on their feet, their Prancing Horse flags flapping like birds on the wing. Scheckter thrust his right forearm from the cockpit and held it rigid in salute. He flowed past the official who, positioned almost mid-track, cleaved the air with the chequered flag. In a few moments Scheckter would be up on the presentation platform, and the crowd below out of control. The police waded in with batons and riot-shields. The crowd hardly noticed, not even someone with blood cascading down their face. *Jo-dee, Jo-dee, Jo-dee* they chanted. Scheckter was Ferrari's seventh World Champion and clearly there would be many more.

On wet days at the kart track Michael would plead 'let me drive'

On rainy days at Horrem, when nobody wanted to go out onto the kart track, Michael would plead 'come on, let me drive, let me drive.' He was lean, slightly angular, but he had balance. He savoured playing around with a kart, loved pitching it into 360-degree turns. There was a problem however. Far in the future he'd remember, 'we were quite poor, to be honest. When I was 10 we didn't even have the money to continue karting.' The fledgling career was saved because Rolf started a modest business renting karts.

Scheckter lingered at Ferrari in 1980, the car a disappointment. Even Villeneuve could only wring a couple of fifth and sixth places from it. But the Italians surrendered then, surrendered to Villeneuve's bravery and brio and brava-do. In him they saw an expression of themselves: live for the moment alone.

Along the side-street at Horrem, middle class sensibilities were irritated by the angry howling which go-kart engines made. The residents decided to enforce noise abatement and the karters departed, leaving the little track to become overgrown. Of a weekend, model cars would be raced round it by remote control: much quieter, much more in keeping with suburban decorum.

The Italian Grand Prix, at Imola in September of 1980, somehow typified Ferrari's descent. Villeneuve's rear tyre exploded early in the race, flinging him into a crash so heavy that he was concussed and temporarily blinded. Scheckter, who'd jarred his neck in final qualifying, slogged on to the finish, which he reached a lap behind the winner.

Three days after Imola, karters gathered at Nivelles, a circuit 20 miles south of Brussels, to contest their own World Championship. An interesting gathering, it included Ayrton Senna. The 11-year-old was taken by his parents to watch – Nivelles was no great distance from Kerpen – and ever afterwards he'd be asked if this was when it all really began. He'd say no, I was still a kid, I was just watching. He must have seen, among the karters hammering round, a quiet, polite Italian called Ivan Capelli who would, when he was drawn to the taming, be almost broken by it. He might have seen Senna being punted off in a late round but wouldn't have seen Senna imploring a British official, Alan Burgess, to find some way to get him re-instated and when Burgess couldn't, bursting into tears. Burgess remains unsure whether this was genuine emotion or a last attempt at re-instatement. None could doubt however that Senna had strong and sometimes overwhelming emotions, as the 11-year-old would one day find out – physically. Anyway, the family drove back from sleepy Belgium to Kerpen after a good day out.

In 1981, Villeneuve conjured two victories from the Ferrari, an extraordinary feat, while his new team-mate Didier Pironi settled in. Pironi was a stylish Parisian with a taste for beautiful women. In a racing car he was hard, ambitious and, at least once, unprincipled. He thought he was the one chosen to tame the Horse.

There was a proper kart track at one of Kerpen's little communities, Manheim. The track was set in countryside, in a bowl scoured by open-cast mining. It had a slightly pastoral feel and one of the corners flowed round a copse of tall trees. Rolf went to work there, looking after the track and paddock, renting out karts, and he found a house just up the winding lane from the track, behind the warehouse of a delivery firm. The 12-year-old had an invaluable advantage over other karters. Proximity.

In 1982, at Imola for the San Marino Grand Prix, Pironi betrayed what Villeneuve considered a moral obligation by overtaking him – against team orders – on the last lap when they were running first and second. Villeneuve never spoke to him again. Two weeks later Villeneuve was killed in final qualifying for the Belgian Grand Prix. Three months later Pironi was crippled when he crashed in practice for the German Grand Prix.

The taming passed into the hands of Frenchmen, the urbane Patrick Tambay and the feisty Rene Arnoux. They finished fourth and third in the 1983 Championship and Tambay departed, letting in Michele Alboreto, a delightful man with an elfin smile and the first Italian that Ferrari had hired since Merzario in 1973. The mythology proclaimed that Enzo hadn't hired Italians because he didn't want the risk of Italian blood on his hands, although – inevitably – nobody seems really to have known.

The 14-year-old played a lot of football, did a bit of judo and a lot of karting. Once, he'd recount, he had a choice between a judo competition and the karting, chose the former and quickly realised his mistake. He'd become a racer now and in 1983 drove in the World Junior Championships. He didn't have far to go, just down the hill past the warehouse. The Championships were held at Manheim.

In 1984 Ferrari were as far away as ever.

The track which Rolf Schumacher built next to the one at Kerpen-Horrem. (Author)

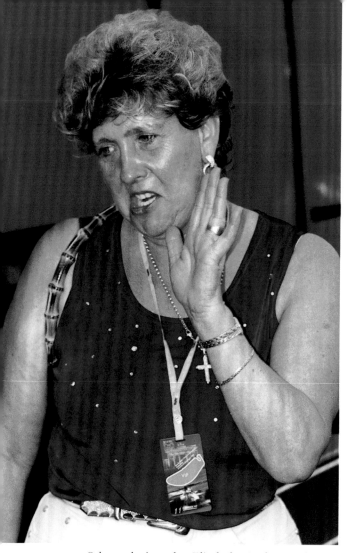

Schumacher's mother Elisabeth. (Andreas Stier)

The 15-year-old won the German Juniors, and everybody seemed to be saying that he was good, very good, but not touched by potential greatness.

In 1985 Alboreto finished second in the Championship, and that was as near as anyone had come since Scheckter.

The 16-year-old was second in the World Juniors at the kart track at Le Mans. That's no guarantee of a golden future but it does argue genuine promise.

In 1986 Alboreto and a pleasant Swede, Stefan Johansson, were lost: Johansson fifth in the Championship, Alboreto joint eighth. Alboreto would stay, Johansson go.

The 17-year-old won the German Seniors and people in single-seater car racing were wondering. Extremely good karters don't necessarily make it in cars. Nobody can ever be sure. The teenager had more mundane considerations

on his mind, like a three-year apprenticeship as a mechanic in a Cologne garage.

In 1987 a genial Austrian with a wicked armoury of practical jokes, Gerhard Berger, partnered Alboreto. Berger liked Enzo and Enzo liked Berger and they talked about girls, a subject with whom they were both intimately connected. Berger scored a couple of victories late in the season to be fifth in the Championship and promised to be the chosen one – or was it just another turn in the cycle of new beginnings which led nowhere? Alboreto was seventh and would stay another year then leave, his energy seemingly exhausted. By now a gifted designer, John Barnard, had come to Ferrari – or rather not come. He'd design the new cars from the calm of his UK base in Guildford, Surrey.

The 18-year-old, beginning to fill out and sometimes sporting a tiny moustache, was good enough to win the European Seniors and at the tail end of 1987 a former karting mechanic, Peter Sieber, gave him a run in a Formula Ford 1600 car at Hockenheim. The sudden transition can be thoroughly disconcerting but the teenager made it go fast and astonished Sieber because he was able to 'tell me what he felt in the car. I thought "oh, he feels a lot of things in the car, he doesn't just drive it."' The teenager had not been on a breathless carousel ride. He'd tamed it.

In 1988 Berger was third in the Championship, Alboreto fifth and going to Tyrrell. In five years at Ferrari he'd won three races. Ferrari had consumed what should have been his years of plenty.

The 19-year-old was noticed by Gustav Hoecker, a man building his own car for a junior category, Formula Koenig. 'The problem facing me was that time was short, literally two weeks to the first race of 1988. I'd seen his promise in karts, I'd seen what I thought was potential. I rang him and he was delighted.' Of the 10 rounds, Michael won nine. He was determined, modest, and thought about what he was doing. He also did some Formula Ford 1600 races, one of them at Salzburg. A Formula 3 team owner, Josef Kaufmann, watched. 'It was wet and I saw one of the drivers was fantastic but I didn't know him. I got a programme and looked. I thought "there is one very, very good driver."' Late in the year he got an offer to drive a Formula 3 car. It wasn't made by Kaufmann, however, but someone called Willi Weber.

In 1989 Nigel Mansell came to partner Berger and soon enough would be called Il Leone – the lion. He won his first race for Ferrari, in Brazil, and priests in Modena came out to ring church bells. The mythology proclaims it happened thus, anyway, and surely it did. Mansell finished the season fourth, Berger seventh and going to McLaren. Alain Prost would be the next. He'd spent six lush seasons at McLaren winning three of his four world titles there but, as McLaren boss Ron Dennis sensed with great clarity, the attraction of being the tamer proved too strong.

The 20-year-old moved up into German Formula 3 with Weber. They'd be together from this time on, Weber as manager and confidant. It was a strong field, including Heinz-Harald Frentzen and Karl Wendlinger. The season finished in an agony of suspense: one point separated the winner – Wendlinger – from the two losers.

In 1990 Prost, precise, prudent and driving a Barnard car of real capability, got as near to succeeding Scheckter as anyone. He conjured a wonderfully evocative phrase about winning at Ferrari – it produced 'a crisis of optimism.' He forced the Championship to the second last round in Japan, where he and Senna crashed. Mansell was fifth, and going back to Williams. Barnard was leaving too.

Michael made an imperious sweep across the German Formula 3 season, winning it cleanly with a clutch of victories, pole positions and fastest laps. A journalist, Wolfgang Schattling, covered the races. 'The second season in Formula 3 he was outstanding. He was mature, experienced, a young guy with an old head. He was shy, introverted … very straightforward. He didn't get into discussions with you but told you his opinion and that was it.' The next step – the last step – towards grand prix racing was Formula 3000 but he didn't go there. He went to Mercedes in the World Sportscar Championship, which might have been more of a cul de sac than a detour. He felt that his career would profit from being with a big company and he was not wrong. He'd reflect: 'I learnt quite a bit in karts, about confidence, about the way that I can prepare overtaking manoeuvres

Schumacher in the early days, with manager Willi Weber. (Andreas Stier)

– but mostly I learned through the series I did when I came into formula racing, and particularly Mercedes, because that was a very good school.' He'd a youthful face and hair down to his collar, both of which 21-year-olds are entitled to have.

In 1991 Jean Alesi, of Sicilian extraction but French by upbringing (an explosive combination), came and was seventh in the Championship. Prost was fired. He'd been criticising Ferrari, something which only ever ends one way: the door is over there.

Looking a man now – not broad, but fit and strong – Michael coped nicely with the weight and power of the Mercedes sportscar, and if he did not have intuitive speed he worked out how to go fast. In August, Eddie Jordan had a vacancy for the Belgian Grand Prix, contacted Weber and next thing the 22-year-old was cycling Spa learning the corners. It impressed the Jordan team: that he'd thought ahead, worked out what he might need, brought a bicycle in the boot of his car. They were more impressed when he worked out a way of coping with two bad bumps on the track and was slightly bemused that everybody else wasn't doing the same. In the Sunday morning warm-up he was fourth quickest, a whisker slower than Senna but quicker than Prost and Alesi. Nothing would ever be the same again. That he cooked the clutch at the start of the race didn't matter overmuch. After an intense political struggle he was in the Benetton for the next race, Monza, where he finished fifth. He'd stay at Benetton another four years.

In 1992 Ivan Capelli joined Alesi and did not endure to the end of the season. He complained that the team didn't support him but, as someone observed, he was 'completely overwhelmed.' A neat little Italian, Nicola Larini, came in to replace Capelli. Alesi was seventh in the Championship, Capelli joint twelfth, and Larini didn't score a point. Something else happened. Barnard re-joined in the middle of this season.

'It's a very long and difficult story,' he will say. 'They had a car which was fairly disastrous but it wasn't just that. They'd been on a slope since 1991, cruised slowly downhill until they arrived at 1992 and

asked me to go back. I was very nervous about that because I knew what could happen and I expressed it very clearly.' This was to Luca di Montezemolo, President of Ferrari. 'We had lots of meetings. I said "look, last time I was here I was in charge of everything and you can't run it from England, don't make that mistake again. If you want me back, let me set up a complete facility in England where I can design – and even build – a prototype. Then we can be working ahead." You need a team in Italy who can run the car and develop it.' Harvey [Postlethwaite,

On and off the track in German Formula 3 in 1989. Schumacher with his then girlfriend Steffi and the mechanic Peter Sieber ... and (nearest the camera) going wheel to wheel with team-mate Frank Schmickler. (Andreas Stier)

himself a designer] was in Italy and they even arranged for Harvey and I to sit down and have a talk because there had been a lot of *history* between Harvey and myself the previous time I was at Ferrari. I said "look, you run the car, you develop it and I'm going to look down the road." That was the deal.'

The 23-year-old was third in the Championship in the Benetton. He'd upset Senna so much in testing at Hockenheim that Senna 'grabbed me by the collar – probably to give me a little message.' He was unintimidated, as you can tell by those words. He'd won Belgium, so near to Kerpen that it felt like his home circuit. His only regret was that his mother hadn't been there. 'Perhaps that is why I felt so emotional. I have to admit I really did cry after Spa.' At 23 years and 240 days he was the fourth youngest race winner.

In 1993 Berger returned to partner Alesi and they managed 28 points between them after what Barnard describes as 'a fairly horrendous year. These were the days of active suspension and we had been wildly left behind. It was "we've got to put an active suspension on there in next to no time" – which you couldn't do: horrendous trying to sort it out, and by now Harvey had gone so there was no person in Italy really to do what we originally said.'

> **I was told, if you really get on with him then the sky's the limit**

The 24-year-old scored 52 points, worth fourth place in the Championship. He was travelling consistently fast and becoming faster, poised to make Benetton a major team.

In 1994 the Ferrari improved, and Berger and Alesi totalled 65 points although few would remember that; or that Alesi was injured early on and Ferrari reached for Larini again. He did two races, crashed immediately in the Pacific at Aida and finished second at Imola. But Imola was shadowland. Senna was killed; also the Simtek rookie Roland Ratzenberger. It is painful to pass by that awful climactic so swiftly, and it had an inescapable relevance. Senna was widely regarded as the best driver in the world. Could Schumacher now become that?

Meanwhile Barnard was held in the contradiction he had tried so hard to avoid: being in Guildford methodically mapping the car of the future while also needing to be hands-on in Italy.

A tumult of a season with Benetton: rancour over an ignored black flag at Silverstone, controversy over an illegality on the car at Spa, a two-race ban, appearances and appeals at the FISA headquarters in Paris; then Adelaide, the race that decided the Championship, and the crash with Damon Hill which pitched Schumacher into the air. It was a bitter, suspect, bizarre thing because Schumacher had just run into a wall and, returning to the track, moved over on Hill. Anyway, at 25 years, 10 months and 10 days he was the second youngest World Champion. There was a hardness about him, although whether that created the climate for the controversies or brought them in its wake nobody could say for sure. Perhaps he didn't know himself. Yet the almost complete control he exercised over a racing car – in certainty of touch, tactical awareness, gun-fighter reflexes, cold analysis, keeping strength in reserve – was profound to behold. Most drivers hate the wet: revealingly, he loved it.

In 1995 Alesi scored 42 points and Berger 31, fifth and sixth in the Championship. Year upon year they rode but never reached the finishing post first. Alesi suffered enough misfortune to break a heart but kept forcing whatever car Barnard gave him to the edge, and over it. His passion flowed into that of the crowd, and theirs flowed back to him in a communion. It was just the sort of thing the mythology created – but Jody Scheckter was still the last Ferrari champion, and that hot, dry Monza afternoon when they chanted *Jo-dee, Jo-dee, Jo-dee* was a long memory ago.

Barnard evaluates the car of 1995 as 'actually quite nice, the 412 was a good little car, simple, basic. Alesi and Berger liked it. What we needed to do was improve the aerodynamic efficiency. One problem I had was that I kept being pushed by Montezemolo. "What are you going to do for us, what's new?" I shouldn't have succumbed to it but they wanted me to produce the miracle. "Where's the miracle?" They wanted something new, something different and *I* kept pushing to try and find it.'

The 26-year-old won nine races, which gave him his second Championship with a furlong or two to spare. He was only the sixth driver in the history of F1 to win the title two years running.

Barnard explores the background. 'It was a case of this: you knew you wanted him, everybody wanted him – he was thunderingly quick – but how do you get him? I was there and at the time I was a strong enough pull. He was interested to work with me and we had programmes going at Ferrari. He went right above di Montezemolo, he went straight in up to Agnelli level [Gianni Agnelli, head of Fiat which owns Ferrari]. He wasn't about to put himself in a situation where the President was changed after a year, which could happen very easily. He and his people made very sure about that.'

The idea was that the miracle would come from driver and designer working together. Barnard insists a driver like that 'wouldn't move unless he thought there was a chance of doing something with a team he was moving to.' Barnard is being factual, not fanciful, when he adds that although they hadn't worked together before 'he'd seen lots of evidence of what I'd done – he'd come to Benetton after I was there – and I'd got a reasonably good track record. I think he was keen to work with me. In fact that was in his contract at the beginning.' If Barnard left, he could leave too.

'It was strange because various people were talking to me saying "well, of course, if you get on with him, if you really work well with him, the sky's the limit". That was true but the problem

The interweaving of the Ferrari dynasty. Schumacher here in 1999 with Jacky Ickx. (Andreas Stier)

Schumacher's indoor kart track at Kerpen, 1999. (Author)

remained, and they didn't realise it: I did not expect to be and did not want to be on track 100 per cent of the time looking after one driver. As everybody knows, I live here in Guildford and I do not intend to move.'

Barnard had spent decades in the jostle, bustle and elbowing of the pit lanes of the world coping with the crisis of the moment, whatever it happened to be. Now others could handle the present. His contribution would be the future.

Some time after the fifth of those nine wins in 1995 – Hockenheim – something almost inevitable happened.

Ferrari offered Michael Schumacher $25 million a year to tame the Horse.

He said yes. Ultimately, it was as simple as that.

chapter two

The rain in Spain (1996)

A November morning. Michael Schumacher flew in his Citation 2 plane from Nice to Bologna with his wife Corinna and a friend. The twin-jet plane had eight seats, cost $1.9m and had belonged to former Formula 1 driver Thierry Boutsen. It was flown by Schumacher's pilot, an American called Roger Giadone. Corinna and friend set off into Bologna to do some shopping while Schumacher was driven to Maranello, 40km to the north west, by Weber.

They toured the Ferrari factory, then Schumacher had lunch with his new partner, Ulsterman Eddie Irvine, and Luca di Montezemolo. Irvine had signed a contract which bound him tightly to supporting Schumacher, not supplanting him. The consolation came in regular wage packets of large amounts. 'I have to tell you Eddie was very happy with his situa-

Ferrari: the wall behind Enzo's desk. (Andreas Beil/ATP)

tion,' Barnard says. 'I'd been involved in that discussion: who do we get as a second driver?'

Schumacher became so engrossed in conversation with the engineers that he was 90 minutes late for a Press Conference. There, Jean Todt presented the two drivers. Schumacher wore blue jeans and a thigh-length anorak, Irvine a casual jacket.

One report, by Pino Allievi contained these words: *The atmosphere in the team was said to be one of curiosity, but not particularly*

Schumacher's first drive in the Ferrari, at Estoril in December 1995. Because he was still contracted to Benetton and there would be conflicting sponsorships he wore plain white overalls. (Formula One Pictures)

warm. Allievi explains, that was the initial feeling about Schumacher. 'We did not know him.'

There had been the opposite of warmth from ordinary Italians during the Grand Prix at Monza a couple of months before. Monza has a paddock like a fortress and an animated crowd stands ten or twenty deep at the entrance yearning for a glimpse of any driver, but especially the two riding the Horses. The trick for the driver is to be as anonymous as possible and get inside the fortress as fast as possible.

Alesi responded to such notions by arriving in the most publicly visible, and touchable, way – on his scooter. The people who'd chanted *Jo-dee, Jo-dee, Jo-dee* so long ago now chanted *Ale-si, Ale-si, Ale-si.*

Schumacher came in a car protected, as one source puts it, by a 'machine gun-toting police escort' and some of the throng called obscenities as he passed. The *tifosi*, the adoring supporters, are prey to emotion more than logic.

They'd treasured Lauda for his heroism and his Championships, flung rotten fruit at him in 1977 because he was leaving Ferrari; they'd thrown stones at Alain Prost and spread straw on the track during testing – so he'd go off – because his Renault was beating the Ferraris; they'd cheered Rene Arnoux, whose Renault had just won the 1982 Italian Grand Prix, because he was joining Ferrari; they'd jeered Riccardo Patrese, a fellow *Italian*, because his Brabham went off leading the 1983 San Marino Grand Prix, allowing a *Frenchman*, Patrick Tambay, to win in a Ferrari. The dislike of Prost was so intense that, this same year of 1983, he arrived with the President of France's bodyguard to protect him; seven years later, when Prost came to tame, they openly venerated him. And so it went. The reaction of the *tifosi* was not fickle or contradictory but entirely consistent. If you were with Ferrari you might win their respect but what they really sought, in Allievi's delicious phrase, was 'people who have something to transmit from the heart.' And if you weren't with Ferrari you represented the enemy.

Mario Andretti understood that perfectly when he was brought back to contest Monza in 1982, replacing Pironi. He'd last driven for Ferrari a decade before and was presently in IndyCars. Andretti wore a red Ferrari cap, Prancing Horse prominent, as he disembarked from an Alitalia jet in Milan. It meant *I care enough about this to show you I care*, it meant *I have come to be the expression of your passion*. The glimpse of the cap created hysteria.

Schumacher could easily silence the obscenities by winning in a Ferrari, and everybody knew that. But he might never

> **When he tried the car we thought 'bloody hell, this is a bit different'**

enter those darkened, secret places every Italian holds sacred because as a matter of first principle he thought, lived and drove rationally. The ones who'd transmitted from the heart – Villeneuve, perhaps Arnoux, certainly Alesi, perhaps Mansell – had driven in the grip of their own passion, offering the blood red cars and themselves as flourishes against whatever fate brought. That created communion.

Nigel Stepney, Ferrari's Chief Mechanic, was present when Schumacher first came to the factory for a seat fitting. Stepney has spent a lifetime in Formula 1, working at Lotus with Ayrton Senna, and sees everything with a steady eye. 'I didn't know Schumacher before,' he says. 'It was the first time he came to Maranello. We prepared him in the November. I was doing the seat fitting with some of the other people, the engineers and everybody. My first impression? Well, he's a very typical German. I say typically German because he's fresh, cold, clean, got a good image – a clean image – and he commands respect. He was very fit and very enthusiastic even for one of the top line racing drivers.'

It really began on another November day, in 1995, at the test track at Fiorano, when Schumacher prepared to lever himself into a Ferrari for the first time. He wore plain white overalls. Alesi and Berger had gone to Benetton. Normally drivers' contracts run to the last minute of the last day of December but, just this once, it made sense to allow Schumacher to test the Ferrari and vice versa for Alesi and Berger. To avoid the nightmare of clashing sponsors, all three dressed down.

It was a cool afternoon and an estimated 2,000 spectators pressed against Fiorano's perimeter fence to witness the moment. Irvine watched too. Schumacher said emotion touched him that so many had come. He covered one lap before a driveshaft problem halted him. They worked on that and the shadows of early evening were drawing in when he put together a sustained but prudent run of 16 laps.

He didn't push it, and that was interesting because mythology demanded that each new leading Ferrari driver break the Fiorano lap record. Schumacher clearly did not feel the need. 'I just wanted to get used to the car,' he'd say before making all the right noises, about how proud he was, about his enthusiasm and the work to be done ('a lot but I am quite optimistic'). He'd explain how he anticipated race wins in 1996 but the Championship wouldn't come into play until 1997. This was the Press Release-speak, the words dried and choreographed: it's how he communicates.

He tested at Estoril and at the end of the first day it rained. Out he went, loving it, then pronounced the Ferrari was the best car he'd driven in the wet. During the test, over four days, he did push – to within touching distance of the fastest man there, Jacques Villeneuve (Williams-Renault). Villeneuve did a 1m 20.94s, Schumacher a 1m 21.20s.

Estoril revealed a potentially serious problem. 'I'd not spoken to him before, not really,' Barnard says. 'We had two cars at the test, the 12-cylinder – the one we'd been racing – and the first 10-cylinder 'mule' [workhorse] that we'd put together. Schumacher came along and drove the 12-cylinder, and of course first thing he was immediately quicker than Alesi and Berger, he was on the pace with the current latest crop of other cars testing at Estoril. He said "I like this, it's a good little car. If I'd had this I'd have won the Championship easily." That's what he said. So we thought "bloody hell, this is a bit different."

'What came out of it was interesting. Through all the season we'd been dealing with the 12-cylinder engine and it had a lot of internal friction in it. Our drivers were finding it difficult to drive smoothly because of this internal friction. Every time you lifted off the throttle you'd get a big reaction from the engine and it would tend to upset the car. We were always struggling with this. Schumacher, on the

The soul of Maranello: Enzo Ferrari's office. (Andreas Beil/ATP)

They'd build an apartment for Schumacher at Maranello. (Andreas Beil/ATP)

other hand, drove a car very differently and it was the first insight I'd had into seeing just how differently. We thought "oh, he'll get in the 10-cylinder and it will be better," because the engine had less friction inside it, it was smoother to drive. You could lift off and it didn't have the massive reaction, and so on and so on. It was lighter at the back of the car and that would help.

'Not so. In fact Schumacher preferred the 12 because he drove it on the throttle and that's what I didn't understand until I was there. He had a front end that would turn into a corner like a go-kart: just flick it in and you're gone through the corner. What he did, he balanced the car on the throttle all the way through the corner and he needed the braking power of the engine to make the car react to the throttle.

There was no way he would even try to see another point of view

'The other guys had been saying *oh Christ, can't drive like this, every time you lift off it does this and it does that* so we'd been working on all kinds of strategies and electronics and goodness knows what. Then along comes Schumacher and says "yeah, I like that."'

Schumacher liked any car set up so that it turned in to corners with vicious suddenness. 'I think the main ability I have is a good and consistent feeling for the limit and I am able to run the car virtually 100 per cent on the limit. That's probably the difference in style.' He'd explain that a driver might have the ability to do that in the entry of a corner but not, say, in midcorner or at the exit again, or combinations of these. 'I can almost do this all the way around the corner.'

Hence the problem for Barnard.

'By this time [the Estoril test] we had already gone down the road for the 10-cylinder, which was the correct decision anyway, but because of that we had to put a seven-speed gearbox in,' Barnard says. 'Schumacher wanted that braking capability and to get it he would run the corner in a higher gear. He said *I need seven speeds because I need to be able to select exactly the gear I want through the corner, therefore giving myself the engine braking: if I can run the engine at high revs I've got more engine braking – because there's more friction. And of course coming out of the corner with the revs up you are already nearer the peak power.*'

A grand prix is about gaining fractions and amassing them so that the fractions become chunks.

'Where I fell foul of him really,' Barnard says with his customary candour, 'is that my experiences working with guys like Alain Prost and Niki Lauda and John Watson was that to make a quick car you needed it to work off the back. In other words, you had the aerodynamic load on the back wheels and effectively all the front wheels did was turn it into the corner. Prostie was the absolute 180 degree opposite of Schumacher and I have to say I think Prost was right, because time in a car is about having enough traction, grip and so on. You cannot underestimate the Prostie capability. John Watson used to tell me *look, I want the car to work from the back, I want to feel as if the back is nailed to the ground and then I'm not worried at all about the car. I can flick the car in.*

'It was very, very difficult to get a car to work like that, and where I was unfortunate with Schumacher was that I wanted to try to do it. In a way that's really where we fell apart – about working the way I thought, off the back of the car and a low downforce front end with a lot of mechanical grip. I thought *he's good enough, he's got such fundamental reactions and just natural driving skills.* All the things that come naturally he'd got, but of course what he also had was a German brain. That meant there was no way he was even going to attempt to see another point of view. I thought *blimey.* It was an immediate problem, and this is before we ever get to 1996.'

Stepney explores this dimension. 'He drives a racing car like a kart. He does a lot of practising on karts at his track in Kerpen. There's a circuit just over the

Italian border from Monaco – Ventimiglia – and I know the guy who runs the place. Michael practised there a lot. He'd go with some friends and two or three karts. All the drivers do their exercises to keep fit and so on, but at the end of the day he still drives a kart. I don't think many of the other drivers do that. He hasn't lost that and I think it's how he makes comparisons, keeps himself concentrated and pushing. I don't know but there's *something* there. And it's good for fitness too. I can't think of many other drivers I have known who've done that all the time.'

The new car, the F310, was launched in mid-February. New car launches are ritualistic, especially at Ferrari where, amidst the pomp and circumstance, the same question comes back. *Is this the year?* Di Montezemolo dealt with it diplomatically. 'Ferrari is coming from a very long road but today we must say that we have reasons to be optimistic.'

The ritual is replaced by reality at the first race of the season. That was the **Australian** Grand Prix on 10 March. Schumacher qualified on the second row of the grid, behind Irvine. After the race had been re-started – Martin Brundle (Jordan) crashed – Schumacher ran fourth, Jacques Villeneuve leading from his Williams team-mate Damon Hill, Irvine third. Irvine obeyed his contract and moved aside, Schumacher dug deep to get within 0.749 seconds of Hill but you could see the Ferrari twitching and bucking under the demands he made of it. After 11 laps the front-runners ran equidistant. At lap 20 Schumacher pitted and rejoined fourth.

Pit stops for refuelling had been part of racing for a couple of years and a team could make as many as they wanted. It had altered grand prix racing completely, introducing tactics which the team could deploy rigidly or alter to suit the unfolding events. At Ferrari, Schumacher (and

Irvine, the loyal team-mate (Formula One Pictures)

The place which would become so familiar, the test track at Fiorano complete with its own petrol station for fast refuelling. (Andreas Beil/ATP)

subsequently Ross Brawn) became artists at exploiting the permutations. Stepney explains that 'the teams are under so much pressure now, they're putting each other under that pressure not only driving on the circuit but in the pit stops as well. You win or lose a race on a pit stop, and it never used to be so critical.'

At Melbourne Schumacher was on a two-stop strategy. The Williamses weren't. Schumacher had been running with a low fuel load, and could only stay with them when it was lighter.

No matter. His brakes were failing and he pitted again on lap 31 to see what could be done, sat in the cockpit explaining while, all around, the mechanics toiled. He was stationary for more than a minute, his race destroyed. He went back out but into a right-hander churned wisps of smoke as the wheels locked. The car coasted gently over a narrow ribbon of grass and he let it reach towards a multi-coloured tyre wall, twisted it and brought it to the track again, dust billowing; returned quietly to the pits and the mechanics wheeled the car into the darkness.

Schumacher returned to Italy to test at Fiorano, working on the difficulties which Melbourne had revealed, then qualified on the second row again in **Brazil.** The Ferrari was, as someone observed, 'evil to drive' but the race would be wet and that might offer an advantage. He made a slow start, sixth, and moved up to fifth but couldn't catch Rubens Barrichello (Jordan). Barrichello and Alesi swooped places and Schumacher bided his time. A dry line appeared and he kept moving off it, scouring the last of the standing water to stop the wet tyres overheating. Frentzen (Sauber) stole up behind him. Along the start-finish straight Barrichello ducked out from behind Alesi and they ran abreast towards the first corner, a corkscrew left.

Schumacher thrust the Ferrari between them as they dipped into the clutches of

He'd run second in Argentina but the rear wing failed. (Formula One Pictures)

the corkscrew, couldn't slice through. Into the right-hander which pitched the cars out of the corkscrew Alesi and Barrichello almost touched. Instantaneously he was hard inside, searching to overtake them both, but he lacked the acceleration. Approaching the left-hander along the mini-straight after that he emerged from

behind them and, abandoning the security of the dry line, tried again but still lacked the acceleration. He retreated to safety, waited.

Frentzen probed for an opening, didn't find one. Schumacher pitted on lap 24, took on wet tyres and they sliced through the pools along the pit lane. When the main weight of the pit stops were done – Schumacher made a second stop on lap 40, changing now to dry tyres – he ran third behind Hill and Alesi. There were tensions towards the end, Barrichello on the attack and overtaking him into the corkscrew.

The corkscrew pitched Barrichello, and

Schumacher sailed stately inside him, resumed in third place as if nothing at all had happened in between.

Hill lapped him and confessed to a 'wry smile' that he'd been able to do that unhindered after all the crashing and bashing of 1994 and 1995. Afterwards, sitting alongside Hill, Schumacher described being lapped as 'not very nice' and smiled sincerely, no irony anywhere. 'Obviously the weather conditions didn't do well for us and put our strategy back a bit. I don't know why but after my first stop, when I got a fresh set of rain tyres, the balance wasn't as good as it had been before. As soon as I went to dry tyres I picked up the pace again. I looked good but nevertheless there is a lot of work in front of us.'

Di Montezemolo was less kind. He was quoted as saying: 'I am deeply unsatisfied by the chassis made by Barnard. I was expecting more performance.'

The pressure was gathering.

Qualifying for the **Argentine** Grand Prix at Buenos Aires seemed to confirm it, Schumacher muscling the car onto the front row of the grid alongside Hill who had pole. 'First of all,' Schumacher would say, 'we need to go into the wind tunnel to find the areas in which we must improve.'

He made a good start to the race by nestling in behind Hill, Alesi third. He began to press Hill, forcing him to fastest lap after fastest lap but the order at the front endured through the first pit stops: Schumacher summoning one of his sprint laps to ensure Alesi didn't get out in front of him.

The safety car patrolled after Pedro Diniz (Ligier) and Luca Badoer (Forti) crashed. When it withdrew Hill pulled away almost immediately and ran over debris from the crash, helplessly churning it at Schumacher. 'I saw something black

> ## You design the car round him, which is OK as long as he is with the team

Anguish at Monaco after he crashed on the first lap. (Formula One Pictures)

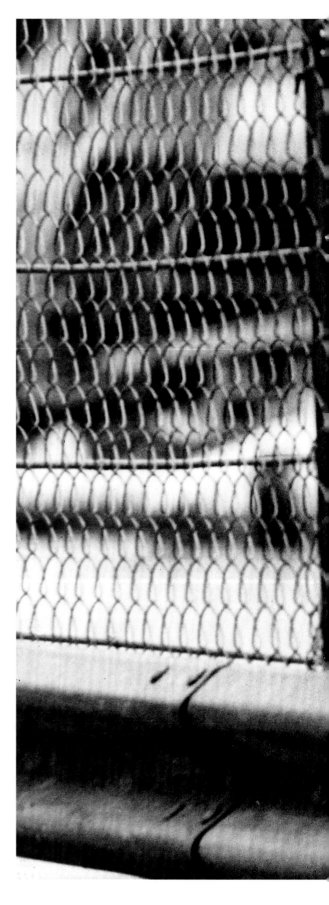

47

flying towards me and instinctively I ducked because I thought it was going to hit me in the face.' Alesi, tracking Schumacher, saw the impact of the debris on the Ferrari's rear wing and rang his own team to tell them to go and alert Ferrari but the on-board radio wasn't clear.

'Soon afterwards,' Schumacher would say, 'the car got loose and I realised something was wrong.' Suddenly he was touring, his rear wing breaking up.

The pressure continued to mount on Barnard, who was quoted as saying that di Montezemolo's comments were 'disruptive' and 'unhelpful.' He also said he was 'fed up with the pantomime' at Ferrari. Reflecting now, Barnard says 'it is true, it is true. Ferrari have got ways of getting rid of people which you can't imagine. A story comes up in an Italian paper or magazine or something like that – theoretically nothing to do with anybody but somebody's written something and it's all being

The first great drive for Ferrari as he exercises absolute mastery over the rain in Spain and every other driver on the track. (Formula One Pictures)

fed, it's all being leaked. They operate like a grand opera and the country is the stage, not the factory: the *whole country* is the stage in the magazines and newspapers...'

Mind you, Ferrari pointed out that di Montezemolo's original comments were inaccurate and reiterated what he had actually said. 'I was expecting more from the F310 but I am quite satisfied with the beginning of this season. We are just behind Williams. My objective for 1996 is to win one more race than in 1995. In Formula 1 you cannot win from day-to-day.'

Di Montezemolo went public at the Nürburgring, where the **European** Grand Prix was being held, giving his support to Barnard. 'I would like to emphasise strongly that I am the man who hired Barnard for Ferrari.' He spoke of the work to be done and said 'I am very pleased to have Barnard with me rather than with someone else.'

Barnard evaluates the car. 'Unfortunately somewhere along the line we made a mistake in the aerodynamics with the 1996 car. I kept asking my aero

Crossing the line to complete the consummate win in Spain. (Formula One Pictures)

guys to check it out. When we did full-size testing against our wind tunnel work our aero correlation was quite good but you had certain dynamic things going wrong on the track, car bouncing and so on. I am sure it was all to do with dynamic ground effects we got on track which we couldn't see in the tunnel.

'Fundamentally that car had an aero that was so different from the tunnel. We thought we were just making an efficiency step from the 1995 car but on track it behaved so differently. I knew the suspension geometry and all the rest of it was pretty much the same as the '95 car – OK it had a different engine in it, and weight distribution was a little bit different – but it was clearly illuminated as an aerodynamic problem. There were a few things done to the car after a few races which made it a bit better and, to be honest, I'm not quite sure how good or bad it was but all I got was [expletive], I just got the [expletive].

'I think part of that was Schumacher lining up the way to get his people in. Todt didn't want this place [Barnard's research centre] in England, anyway, he said it and he said it to me as well. That was his opinion and I got on with him fine. I didn't have major problems but I knew what was coming. At the same time, there was the constant *barraging* of the car although if you look at the record, at the end of the day it wasn't that bad.

'The way Schumacher drives the car, and the way he likes it, you tend to end up doing a car around him: its balance, its aerodynamics and so on. I'm talking again about the reason it had a 7-speed gearbox, all those things. Before you know where you are, you've got the thing built completely by Schumacher and that's fine so long as Schumacher's still there, but then lose Schumacher and you're …'

Stepney evaluates and broadens the situation, unconsciously echoing Barnard in his conclusion. Schumacher, Stepney says, 'dragged the car round' to good effect. 'If the driver does that, and pulls the team around, everyone *believes,* and it all starts to come together. We were at that point at Ferrari where we weren't quite ready for him – but we'd never have been quite ready for him to come until he did come to help us!'

The broadening: 'He takes you with him, not as much as Senna though. Senna was a lot stronger in that respect. Look at the way he dealt with Honda. He had a lot, lot more pulling power than Michael. That's the feeling I have.'

The echoes: 'The problem is that even though you have the best driver in the world you still have to have the best car. So you have to be careful. Remember McLaren. They built a team round Senna and Senna left and they lost five years in rebuilding. You can end up with all the top drivers like that. You put all your eggs in one basket and somebody drops the basket ...'

At the **Nürburgring** Schumacher 'dragged' the car to third in qualifying and said it felt better than in Argentina. Because this was a season dominated by Williams, he had Hill and Villeneuve in front of him.

He was about to show why he was worth the $25 million.

Villeneuve made a strong start, Schumacher fourth, Hill behind him. On lap 6 Hill took him at the end of the start-finish straight, Schumacher not resisting. Hakkinen (McLaren) came up behind so Schumacher faced twin problems: holding Hakkinen while trying to re-take Hill. Once he almost made it as Hill attacked Barrichello for third place. The pit stops broke all this up and, after them, Schumacher dealt with Coulthard (McLaren), holding the inside line through the left-right sweeping corners to a mighty roar from the crowd. He was third which became second behind Villeneuve when Hakkinen pitted. It was lap 27 of the 67, the gap 8.7 and Schumacher had just set fastest lap. He sprinted.

[Please note that because this is a book about Schumacher, all the columns of gain/loss in the tables of lap times which follow give him precedence, so + means Schumacher gained time and – means he lost it.]

	Schumacher	Villeneuve	Gain
Lap 27	1:21.976	1:46.735	after pit stop
Lap 28	1:21.987	1:23.406	+ 1.419
Lap 29	1:21.822	1:23.130	+ 1.308
Lap 30	1:22.019	1:24.235	+ 2.216

By lap 37 he was directly behind Villeneuve so the second pit stops would decide everything.

He was stationary for 8.5 seconds and regained the track poised for what would need to be two fast laps, but Coulthard happened to be in the way and each melting second he spent behind Coulthard battered the tactic. On these whims of chance are many modern motor races decided, all the technology which money can buy, useless.

Villeneuve pitted and as he moved away Schumacher came like the wind down the pit lane straight, closing but never near enough. Villeneuve retained the lead to the end despite pressure from Schumacher and a clutch of back-markers to negotiate. Villeneuve, so fresh to grand prix racing, cut through them like an old master and Schumacher paid tribute to that. Villeneuve, he said, 'judged all the moves perfectly.'

Arguably only Schumacher could have brought the car to second place 0.762 behind Villeneuve.

'I was thinking the whole time about last year,' Schumacher added, sporting that mouthful-of-teeth grin. He was remembering how, impudently and impossibly, he'd threaded past Alesi at the hairpin in 1995 and 'there should be that situation coming now where I can pass Jacques by making the same move, but obviously he did a fantastic race without mistakes and there was just no way for me to pass. He had the edge on top speed.

The podium in Spain, and the body language reveals everything. (Formula One Pictures)

But we had a great race together, very close fighting and I'm very pleased to finish. In the middle of it I was a bit worried because I got some noise at the back and I thought [GRIMACE] *that's it*, but I was able to finish. I think we have shown that we go step-by-step. Qualifying was really surprising but you'll have to wait a little bit longer until we are back on the winning road. We will, I am sure.'

And so he came to Imola for the **San Marino** Grand Prix, the first 'homecoming,' the first possibility of communion with the *tifosi*. He was quickest on the Friday by half a second and, in a climactic end to qualifying, wrung an astonishing lap of 1m 26.890 seconds from himself (Hill next, 1m 27.105) although immediately after he'd taken pole the rear suspension broke, pitching him into a gravel trap. He did a tour of honour on an open-topped vehicle and waved frantically. 'It feels like I won the race but that's what Italy's like.'

He made a hesitant start to the race, moving to mid-track, the Ferrari shivering as the full power came on. He had Hill to one side, Alesi to the other, Villeneuve behind and Coulthard thrusting forward outside Hill. On the run towards Tamburello corner Alesi put wheels on the grass so Schumacher stole through but Alesi flung the Benetton across the width of the track and tried to retake him on the outside. That was communicating from the heart, that was what the *tifosi* had adored about Alesi.

Schumacher blocked Alesi and braked so hard for Tamburello that he dug smoke from his front right tyre. The order: Coulthard, Hill, Schumacher, then Mika Salo (Tyrrell) who, all but unnoticed, maintained steady progress.

Into Tamburello on the second lap Hill placed the Williams over to the right – the mouth of Tamburello snaking to the left – and Schumacher was inside. For an instant Hill was coming across, realised, swivelled away. Schumacher went through

Precision in Canada but the driveshaft failed.
(Formula One Pictures)

and chased down Coulthard, leant on him but Coulthard pitted. Schumacher led a grand prix in a Ferrari for the first time.

Schumacher conjured a 1m 29.515, fastest so far, and pitted. He was stationary for 9.5 seconds. He'd done enough to keep Coulthard behind him but Hill, who'd inherited the lead when Schumacher stopped, hadn't stopped himself yet and sprinted, set a new fastest lap and built a 20-second cushion. He'd done enough: when he emerged from his stop in the lead it was the defining moment of the race. Schumacher followed him home.

I made mistakes – I'm very sorry for the team, and very angry with myself

On the last lap the Ferrari's right front brake disk exploded, locking the wheel solid. Schumacher rammed the car forward and over the line, smoke seeping from the tyre. The *tifosi* liked this. All right, it wasn't Gilles Villeneuve at Zandvoort all those years ago hauling his Ferrari to the pits on three wheels to get a fourth wheel and rejoin the race, but it was a gesture from the same school of emotions: never say die. When he parked it on the grass at the little left-hander beyond the start-finish straight the *tifosi* flooded on and engulfed him. Communion? They'd probably have done that anyway...

'What happened? A good question. I don't know. Something in the front wheel broke, the bearing or the wheel itself. That was after Aqua Minerale into the chicane and I just had three wheels left to finish with. I was thinking I had to go another full lap [FLEETING GRIN] and I was very lucky and happy that the race was finished when I crossed the line. It wasn't too bad and I just made it. It was [SHRUG] quite interesting.'

The pressure continued to mount on Barnard. 'The problem was this: on the one side these people [Ferrari] had brought us all together thinking "ah, what a combination, we'll get Schumacher and Barnard working together like father and son" sort of thing. It might have been brilliant except for a few difficulties. One, that wasn't what I had intended to do when I came back to Ferrari and two, I suppose we just didn't get on. We just didn't click. You do or you don't, you can or you can't.

'I am very bad at disguising my feelings. If I like somebody I think they feel it, they know it and I have no problems. If I don't get on with somebody they also probably know it. So it was a combination of *I didn't want to be there* and *I didn't really click and get on with him*. I can't say that we really fell out. I think he was surprised that I didn't go to every test and every race and just spend my time working with him but, I thought, once he realised that, he was immediately pushing to get people who he knew would do it, people like Ross Brawn and so on. They would work for Michael and no-one else, and Eddie [Irvine] would make sure the spare car was warmed up and ready to go, basically.'

Schumacher took pole at **Monaco** with a consummate lap half a second quicker than Hill and rationalised that by judging the track conditions must have improved and he'd got himself 'tuned in a little bit better.' A wet race, Hill into the lead, Schumacher – as it seemed – proceeding at a prudent interval behind him. He rounded the Loews hairpin and moved into the descending right-hander after that, riding the red and white kerbing on the inside. As the Ferrari came off this kerbing he felt the car floating away towards the Armco over on the other side. He'd oversteered. In a desperate instant he churned the steering wheel right-right-right to miss the Armco but the car skated on and impacted. 'I made a mistake at the start and I made a mistake here too. I'm very sorry for the team and very angry with myself.'

Like the greats in any discipline, Schumacher had a mental clarity that set him apart: treat every mistake the same way. 1) You analyse how you did it, so you are armed with that knowledge. 2) Using the knowledge, you never do it again. 3) You store it in your mind for reference, but you don't dwell on it because the past is only a sequence of lessons which make the present better. And as it happened, eight years before and not more than 30 or 40 paces away – the next section of Armco, in fact – Ayrton Senna crashed when, leading, he lost concentration. He took good care of 1) and 2) but did dwell on 3) and it took him half a season to shake that off. Schumacher wouldn't permit himself any such introspection. He'd shaken it off exactly two weeks later.

Monaco had been 19 May, the **Spanish** Grand Prix at Barcelona was on 2 June. He qualified third behind Hill and Villeneuve. And here is the next irony, because the race was run in a deluge which made Monaco into a spring shower.

The start went so wrong that he reached for a single word – 'disaster' – before amplifying the sequence of events. 'I went for the clutch and there was nothing. I nearly stalled, then tried it again. For some reason I just had an on/off clutch. Fortunately no-one went into the back of me and I don't know how many positions I lost. Even Diniz [starting seven rows behind] passed me, *I think*. Now I know how it is to start a wet race from the back. You just can't see anything. I was really afraid I'd go into someone.'

The key is *I think*. Imagine standing directly under a raging waterfall and looking up into it wearing goggles. In that, 20 cars were churning and nobody could see much except Villeneuve who, leading, had a clear track ahead. It may be that on this opening lap Schumacher overtook three cars, it may be four. He crossed the line sixth 6.241 seconds behind Villeneuve.

	Schumacher	Villeneuve	Gain/Loss
Lap 1	2: 00.510	1: 54.269	– 6.241

Irvine skimmed off on lap 2 and didn't come back, the car sunk in sodden grass, its rear wheels spinning, and that made Schumacher fifth.

	Schumacher	Villeneuve	Gain/Loss
Lap 2	1: 53.890	1: 52.770	– 1.120
Lap 3	1: 53.408	1: 52.182	– 1.226

Hill skimmed off on lap 4 and did come back – gently coaxing the car forward, not too fast, not too slow – by which time Berger and Schumacher had gone

The grid at Hungary, keeping all your secrets under wraps. (Formula One Pictures)

through; and that was fourth. The gap was out to 8.476, which is how it generally goes when the leader has the clear track and you're peering into the waterfall.

	Schumacher	Villeneuve	Gain/Loss
Lap 4	1: 52.142	1: 52.263	+ 0.121

Schumacher set fastest lap, moved past Berger; and that was third.

Lap 5	1: 50.568	1: 52.598	+ 2.030

He immediately gained on Alesi who was with Villeneuve and trying to apply pressure. Somewhere in the walls of water behind Alesi was the Ferrari – hunting. Alesi was known to be quick and brave in the wet. Alesi was hunting too, hunting Villeneuve.

Lap 6	1: 49.045	1: 52.760	+ 3.715
Lap 7	1: 51.144	1: 52.355	+ 1.211
Lap 8	1: 51.467	1: 51.077	− 0.390

Schumacher drew full up, darted out for a sight, darted back. He loomed over Alesi. He took different lines through the corners. He left his braking late for a left-hander forcing Alesi to concede; and that was second. Immediately he gained on Villeneuve, then drew full up wielding the Ferrari with such dexterity that for him, and him alone, the track might have been dry. On lap 9 the gap was a meaningless 0.458 seconds and three laps later he did to Villeneuve what he'd done to Alesi; and that was first. He set new fastest lap and shed Villeneuve, who subsequently explained that Schumacher had been quicker through all the corners. Now he lapped devastatingly faster than Villeneuve.

Lap 12	1: 47.337	1: 51.078	+ 3.741
Lap 13	1: 46.543	1: 50.247	+ 3.704
Lap 14	1: 45.517	1: 49.426	+ 3.909

The other 50-odd laps? Schumacher drove into his own mythology. In the end he beat Alesi by more than 45 seconds. That seemed both pertinent and irrelevant. Alesi had been in a different race,

Mirror images in Belgium where he prepares to score a brilliant victory. (Formula One Pictures)

and so had the other four who finished, and so had the 14 who failed to finish. More than that, Schumacher was now second equal in the Championship with Villeneuve on 26 points, Hill on 43.

'It's amazing. If anybody would have asked me how much I would have bet on any of this, I wouldn't even have bet a penny on it.'

Next morning *L'Equipe,* the French daily sports newspaper, carried a large heading:

SCHUMACHER, ACE OF ACES

Under it Johnny Rives, their very experienced correspondent, wrote: 'You have to plunge into the history of Formula 1 and examine the grands prix contested under equally difficult conditions to measure the quality of the performance achieved by Michael Schumacher yesterday, setting it against the most famous epic drives.

'Jackie Stewart, at the Nürburgring, in 1968, in the rain and the fog, won by four minutes. In 1972, at Monaco under a deluge, J-P Beltoise held in check Jacky Ickx, considered *the* great master in the wet. Closer to us, there was Alain Prost and Ayrton Senna in 1984 at Monaco again. And this same Senna, at the beginning of 1985, at the Grand Prix of Portugal when he got the first of his 41 victories. Or, yes, Senna again, always him, at Donington in 1993 [at the European Grand Prix where he led by a lap] ...'

Barnard gives a postscript. 'I wasn't in Spain, but I was talking to [Giorgio] Ascanelli, the Chief Engineer. One of the things they did for that race – which other people didn't do, or didn't have available – was put maximum downforce on. I think in those days we pretty much generated more downforce than any of the other cars and that was coupled with Schumacher's amazing skills. He just drove round everybody and it was a classic Schumacher victory.'

Stepney was in Spain and gives another postscript.

Schumacher didn't know how many cars he got past on the first lap.

Waltzing, Spa. (Formula One Pictures)

'You look at Senna in Portugal in 1985 or Donington in 1993. Take Donington. How many cars did Senna overtake? About five on the first corner. Some drivers just adapt quicker.'

What is it?

'Hmmm. I don't know. It's down to ... feeling and confidence, but sometimes you can have too much confidence and then you go off.'

This is an appropriate place to let Stepney evaluate Schumacher.

'He's like all the great ones. There are differences between him and other drivers of other eras – and we are talking about a

completely different era now – but these great ones have something about them. They don't need to push what they have onto the people around them.

'When he came he helped Team Ferrari greatly in this respect: we had a lot of problems and we didn't have a competitive car as such, well, not a very competitive car. The other drivers we'd had caused more disturbance, they didn't calm the waters. Alesi put everything out in the open – in the Press, everything. Michael has never done that and when he started off he took people here by surprise because of it. Personally I'd thought that's how it would be because he's not like Berger and Alesi: they open their mouths and think afterwards. He helped to calm everything down, because he knew he could do the job. He never had self-doubt and I don't think the good ones do have, they are always very positive because they *know* they can. And if you know you can do something, you do it automatically. You don't have to worry about it.

'I like to work with good drivers. The major problem at Ferrari as far as drivers are concerned is that they are baby-sat too much. That hasn't affected Michael as much as some of the other drivers. He's

got the sort of mind that sees through all that and asks *what are we really doing?* He cuts through that crap, he *knows* what he wants.'

Grand prix racing mirrors life in at least one sense. It kicks you when you're up as well as when you're down. **Canada** was downbeat, third on the grid despite a revised version of the F310 but the engine died before the parade lap and he started from the back. He reached seventh but after his pit stop the driveshaft broke.

In **France** he took pole but the engine blew on the parade lap; in the **British** at Silverstone he ran fourth but retired on lap 3 with a gearbox problem and the talk was whether he'd extend his contract beyond 1997. Di Montezemolo weighed in with 'we are extremely pleased with Schumacher and for me it is important that the driver is pleased with Ferrari. We both have the intention of going on together. I would rather pay $20m for Schumacher than the same amount for two drivers.'

In **Germany** he qualified third and complained about the car, finished fourth. In **Hungary** he took pole and led, finished ninth with a throttle problem. The promise of the season, the laying of a foundation for an assault on the Championship in 1997, was ebbing away; and when the races are coming at you in their hectic rhythm every other weekend you can be running as hard as you can just to stay still.

In **Belgium** he qualified third again (behind the Williamses), and this after a major crash on the Friday when he turned in to a left-hander and the car danced away from him, swapped ends, bounced across a gravel trap and smacked the tyre wall high up. He bruised his knee. He made a better start to the race than Hill and crowded Villeneuve, pitching and pounding the Ferrari to stay with him but each lap at the Bus Stop chicane he lost time to Villeneuve.

> ## They radioed him that all would be well if he just kept off the kerbs

He forged fastest lap and pitted first on lap 14 but there was a measure of confusion for spectators and teams alike. The safety car was out...Villeneuve pitted and emerged behind Schumacher ... Coulthard led Hakkinen but neither had pitted ... they were on one-stop strategies. When the safety car pulled off and the racers resumed, Schumacher felt 'a lot of play in the steering.' Spa is imperious in the speeds it allows and, as a consequence, this 'play' frightened him. 'I was close to stopping.' He radioed and the team reassured him that all would be well if he respected the kerbs by staying off them.

The McLarens came in, giving him the lead. He pitted a second time, passing the lead to Villeneuve, who passed it back when he pitted. Villeneuve emerged from his second pit stop as Schumacher was rounding La Source. The pit lane exit is further on down the incline. Villeneuve ducked across the track but Schumacher had the impetus of accelerating from La Source and went clean by. And that was the story of the Belgian Grand Prix. When it was done he conjured an evocative phrase. After the frightener with the steering, to win 'was just Hollywood life.'

A question remained about the **Italian** Grand Prix two weeks away. Would there be communion? How much had been remembered about the armed guard a year ago while Alesi scooted round on a scooter?

Qualifying obeyed the current of the season, third behind Hill and Villeneuve, but you can gain or lose position on the long, sustained surge to the first chicane when the race begins. This chicane is so absurdly tight that a hunting pack of cars braking for it, and *still* trying to create positions, remains an alarming annual spectacle – or even spectre. Imagine a stampede towards cliff's edge. In it Schumacher lost, not gained, and the order completing the opening lap was Hill, Alesi, Hakkinen, Villeneuve, Coulthard, Schumacher.

Alone at La Source hairpin. (Formula One Pictures)

On lap 2 Coulthard spun off; and that was fifth.

Into the Ascari curve he moved past Villeneuve; and that made him fourth, at 4.142 seconds from Hill. He needed to keep that gap more or less constant and did. After the third lap it stood at 4.793.

Hakkinen had run into a loose tyre from one of the silly mini-tyre walls which decorated Monza that year and it broke his nose cone. Schumacher crowded him but Hakkinen had to pit anyway for repairs; and that was third.

Hill set fastest lap and at lap 5 had opened the gap to 5.917.

The *tifosi* enjoyed this theatre, the hunter and the hunted

Next lap Hill clipped one of the mini-walls which set the Williams spinning down the track. He wrestled it until it pointed forwards but the engine had stalled, the suspension bent. Schumacher second. The gap to Alesi was 2.995. Schumacher accelerated and ate into that, to 1.629 on the tenth lap. The *tifosi* appreciated this stretching of their emotions, the hunter and the hunted, Alesi still in their hearts, Schumacher absorbing their minds. Schumacher was impressed with Alesi's straight-line speed which prevented him getting close enough for a proper assault although he carried a heavy fuel load 'so we could stop quite late.' He worried that Alesi might be doing the same. The hunt went to lap 30 when Alesi pitted and Schumacher accelerated:

| Lap 31 | 1: 27.217 |
| Lap 32 | 1: 26.391 |

Schumacher pitted, was stationary for 8.8 seconds (Alesi 9.0) and did retain the lead, won it by 18.265 seconds with only one alarm when he struck a mini-wall hard enough to pluck the steering wheel from his hands. He'd call this a stupid mistake. As he moved towards the line a last time he raised a clenched fist and held it rigid just above the rim of the cockpit, a curiously subdued gesture. Later on round the slowing down lap he began to pump the fist like a piston, but that's the maximum you can convey from a cockpit.

The *tifosi* became a mob. They behaved like this every year. In their thousands they gathered beneath the podium balcony for the anthems, the champagne and the antics. Schumacher said he'd 'never seen so many emotions of so many people enjoying themselves. The way they celebrate is only possible in Italy.' Press Release-speak. He shook his head in bewilderment. When a Ferrari wins here, Monza is many, many things – none of them Kerpen.

Grand prix racing mirrored real life again. **Portugal** kicked a little (fourth on the grid, third in the race), **Japan** less so (third on the grid, second in the race). It gave him 59 points, third in the Championship. Whether Ferrari were making real progress, or whether Schumacher was so good he masked that they weren't, remained unresolved. It would be resolved soon.

Wouldn't it?

chapter three

The wrong thing to do (1997)

Rumours are a permanence at Maranello, delicious or damaging depending on who, what and where you happen to be. The October 1996 crop suggested that Benetton's Technical Director, Ross Brawn, would be coming to Ferrari and by definition that raised questions about Barnard's future, questions heightened because evidently Rory Byrne, Benetton's Chief Designer, would be coming too. The crop flowered into November. Byrne was leaving Benetton but to set up a scuba diving school in Asia while, simultaneously, Brawn was staying at Benetton, joining Ferrari and, for good measure, joining Arrows.

Brawn began work at Ferrari on 16 December, stayed until one in the morning and made Jean Todt stay too. The latest attempt at the taming was under way.

Schumacher extended his contract to the end of 1999 and secured, if you believed even more rumours, a pay rise to $30m per annum.

The new car, the F310B, was described by Barnard as 'conventional.' It was launched at Maranello on 7 January and the Marlboro Press Service caught the mood nicely because, just this once, there was a variation to the ritual: 'Despite thick snow on the ground, heavy rain and near-freezing temperatures, there was a full house when Ferrari President Luca di Montezemolo and drivers Michael Schumacher and Eddie Irvine unveiled their 1997 Formula 1 challenger to 400 press and VIP guests gathered inside a huge tent that had been erected on the Maranello test track.'

Di Montezemolo said: 'The car is ready for two months of work and testing before the season, and the team is now very strong, organised and maintaining continuity. Our drivers are fantastic and I am sure we have a good year ahead of us. I have said it for three years in a row but this sport sometimes makes you wait. The ways of God are complicated, but 1997 will be good.'

Schumacher gave the car some initial testing at Fiorano (31 laps) and made the noises, about how much promise it seemed to have, how small adjustments needed to be made.

Reflecting, Barnard says: 'We thought we had learnt from our mistakes on the 1996 car. It was getting very disruptive by that time because Todt had gone out and hired two aero dynamicists over in Italy and it kind of ruined our programme [in Guildford]. Effectively the development was switched off here and went over there. I think the 1997 car wasn't a bad car at all.'

A few days after the launch, Schumacher was at the ski resort of

Winter wonderland: Schumacher at the traditional week at the Italian resort of Madonna di Campiglio where Formula 1 goes to play ... but skiing isn't always as easy as it looks. (Formula One Pictures)

Madonna di Campiglio, where he met Italian ski slalom champion Alberto 'The Bomba' Tomba and where Irvine went snowboarding. Schumacher was in expansive mood, although never compromising his pragmatism, and he covered a lot of ground.

'Fiorano was beautiful in the snow but with the track so wet comparisons with last year's car are impossible. The F310B conforms to regulations, is easy to drive and hasn't caused any problems. It's a good sign. Reliability will be very useful this season. It's not possible to know whether we can start winning right away. We won't even know after we have tested against our competitors [at Jerez].' No, he added, they'd only really know at the first race, Melbourne on March 9.

Maybe I could have had more fun but I think I made the right choice

He explained that 'a driver can make a technical contribution to the performance of his car. Last season I made a graphic to show how I felt in the car, what worked and what didn't. It was very helpful. We uncovered a lot of problems. But then it's up to the designers to find solutions. Aerodynamically Formula 1 cars are so complex today that even a very small thing may require a design overhaul.'

He also said, astonishingly: 'My teammate Eddie Irvine could not work well last year because we only had one car for testing. This year we will have two.' He illustrated it by pointing out that at Melbourne in 1996 Irvine had let him through on the first lap 'because I was fastest. This year, if Eddie is fastest, I'll have to stay behind for the sake of the team. If he has a better chance for the title, I'll try to help him. He will do the same for me. And, if I have to retire [from races] he'll go for the points.'

The astonishing aspect was that Schumacher had written into his contract that Irvine would behave with the absolute obedience of a Number 2 unless Schumacher happened to be in trouble, in which case, and presumably still at the team's discretion, Irvine would be unleashed.

Irvine, who'd finished tenth in the 1996 Championship with a threadbare 11 points, spoke diplomatically. 'I will do better this year but don't ask me to make any predictions. It wouldn't make sense. I am not a frustrated driver. Lots of people have asked why I haven't complained to Ferrari but I think that, under the circumstances, everybody was doing the best they could in 1996. This year, my job will be to stay as close to Schumacher as I can, even though I am contractually obliged to let him overtake me. I absolutely do not regret leaving Jordan. Maybe I could have had more fun, but from the point of view of my career I think I made the right decision.'

Schumacher went to Jerez, the car suffered three engine failures early in testing – and a fourth later – and his happiness with the car, or lack of it, generated a fresh crop of rumours. These hardened to: exit Barnard, joining Alain Prost at Ligier, enter Byrne, exchanging the delights of the Thai coast for the shark-infested waters of Maranello. Thereby hangs a tale.

'I'd finished at Benetton,' Byrne says, 'and I was in the Far East to start the scuba diving school. I'd worked flat out until seven o'clock of the evening of 31 December at Benetton and early January that was *it*, I was actually on an island right in the south of Thailand having a look at the prospects. I was going to spend a few months sussing out the various areas seeing what the potential was. I was staying in a little guest house right on the beach and the lady who ran the place called me off it. She said there was a bloomin' phone call for me and your first thought is *Jeez, what's going on? Is it bad news of my family back in South Africa or what?* It was Jean Todt on the phone. He said they were looking at restructuring the whole organisation and bringing everything back to Italy and did I fancy the job of Chief Designer? I said "well, I'll think about it."

'The reason he had my number is that of course I'd been quite friendly with Ross

Brawn. I'd left him my phone number and said "if ever you're out there, this is where I'll be staying for the first few weeks. If you fancy a bit of diving, come out!" Obviously when he joined Ferrari he'd given the number to Todt and so I got this call. About ten days later I was in Maranello …'

What was the thinking behind the decision, because it's not like Benetton ringing and saying 'we're in a bit of trouble, can you come back?' This is Ferrari you're talking about.

'The way I figured it, I was being offered the opportunity to design a car which would hopefully win a Championship for Ferrari for the first time in two decades. That is a unique challenge. You only get one such in the world. That was the first thing: I thought about the challenge, and, at the end of the day, there was nothing stopping me doing what I wanted to do [the diving school], I was just delaying it a few years. Then there was the thought of working with Michael and Ross and I thought yes.'

Michael must have been pushing for you.

'I don't know. It's quite possible.'

He was going to surround himself with the people he knew.

'Sure. There must have been an element of that in it.'

Meanwhile, still at Jerez, Schumacher had handling problems. Although he made noises about the improvements already achieved, he ventured coded criticism when he added: not as many as he'd hoped. Berger in the Benetton was fastest at the end of the week with 1m 21.24s, Schumacher seventh on 1m 22.86s.

Barnard remembers Jerez as 'virtually the last thing I had to do with the car. I went down there on the basis of doing a few set-up changes with it and seeing how it was going to perform. The problem was Ross Brawn was there, Ascanelli was there, Todt was there and Schumacher was there. It was impossible. I stayed two days and then went. I said *that's it, I'm finished, I've had enough.* They were doing things which even Ross Brawn was sitting there saying *we shouldn't be doing this.*

'They had an active differential in, and all the experiences I have had of active differentials – over many, many years – is that you are never 100 per cent sure what you've got. You can play with them and

Working lunch, Maranello. (Andreas Beil/ATP)

change a car and you can make a car so bad so quickly with them. The last thing I wanted was a brand new car with an active differential. I said "let's put the standard differential in and work from that." They said "no, no, we know what it does, we are absolutely sure." In the end I thought: this is nonsense, this is ridiculous now, we have got to a farce situation. I could have stood up and said *stop, I have got control of the set-up of the car, I am still here* but I thought, what's the point? I knew it was over, I knew I was going. So I thought, just walk away. I said *there's no point in me staying any longer,* packed my bags and went. That was it, that was the end of it really.'

He's good at knowing if a change will really make the car faster

Meanwhile, Ralf Schumacher joined Jordan, by virtually the same route as his brother. He'd started karting at three, been in club races at six, and became German Junior Champion in 1991. He graduated to cars in Formula 3, did some Japanese Formula 3000 and, towards the end of 1996, tested a McLaren Mercedes.

There had been brothers in Formula 1 before (ten pairs) and, just for the record, eight pairs of fathers and sons, so the Schumachers were by no means unique. However they'd meet in the most direct way and that probably was unusual. Speaking of family, a daughter – Gina-Maria – would be born to Michael and Corinna on 19 January.

Ralf was asked the inevitable questions.

Is it a problem or an advantage to have the same name as the best driver in the world?

'Listen, when the results are there the name has no importance. Clearly I am not able to escape the comparison with Michael but I feel I have the right to be a little slower than he is for the moment.'

Have you had the chance to discuss the racing with your big brother? Do you exchange information?

'No, not really. When we get the chance to talk quietly with each other we prefer to talk about things of everyday life.'

Did Michael help you to get into Formula 1?

'The name Schumacher helped me, that is for sure, but Michael did nothing directly. He half-opened the door but I organised a way through the door on my own. I was the one who spoke to Eddie Jordan. It wasn't Michael.'

At Maranello, Byrne examined his inheritance, the 1997 car. 'Certainly early on it was difficult. I was faced with the car and we had to do two things. 1) build up the design infrastructure in Italy because there wasn't any. The R&D, everything, was in Guildford. We had to recruit most of the technical side of a Formula 1 team *toute de suite* and 2) design a car for 1998 with a very big rule change, so not only did we have to assemble the people but we had to get on with a car.'

Is there anything you can do as a designer when you are confronted with somebody else's car, in this case Barnard's?

'The first thing is try and understand the car. His design philosophy is different to mine, and understandably. All people's design philosophies are different, certainly to some degree. And there were quite a few fundamentals that were different to what I was used to doing. One thing I have learnt is don't steam in and rubbish what's there and try and put bits of your own ideas on because, really, that very seldom works. The first thing you've to do is understand the animal you've got. It took us a while. And there were one or two fundamental errors in the car which fortunately we were able to rectify in a fairly short space of time.'

Ferrari approached the **Australian** Grand Prix as they had approached the first race of every season since Scheckter in 1979, consumed by wondrous uncertainty. As if to minimise this uncertainty Schumacher stressed that the realistic objective for 1997 was to get points, that places on the podium would have to wait. Immediately events contradicted that.

At Melbourne he qualified third behind the Williamses of Villeneuve and his new team-mate Heinz-Harald Frentzen. David Coulthard was alongside him, Eddie Irvine and Mika Hakkinen on the row behind. After a blast of a start – Irvine, rampant, burst down the inside and locked his brakes, went across the track and forced Villeneuve and Herbert off – Frentzen led from Coulthard and Schumacher. Frentzen was on a two-stop strategy and, with a lighter fuel load, drew away but his first stop on lap 17 made him third. He ran there until Coulthard and Schumacher, on one-stop strategies, pitted and returned the lead to him. During Schumacher's stop the rig didn't deliver the full amount of fuel and that forced him to stop again towards the end for a splash'n'dash, as they say. He was stationary for 4.4 seconds. The order – Coulthard, Frentzen, Schumacher – broke up when Frentzen's brakes failed with just three laps to go and he crashed, hoisting Schumacher to second although he'd finish 20.046 seconds behind Coulthard.

'Luckily I started off badly,' he'd say 'otherwise Eddie would have taken me off as well! It's the first race out of 17 and so it doesn't say really a lot. The good thing is that Jacques didn't score points. In my view he will score many this year.'

Schumacher qualified on the front row for the **Brazilian** Grand Prix at Sao Paulo (Villeneuve pole) and made a strong start into that corkscrew left-right at the end of the pit lane straight. Villeneuve moved to the theoretically commanding position of mid-track but Schumacher thrust the Ferrari down the inside and, as the corkscrew lured them in, they were abreast, Schumacher holding the advantage of the inside. Villeneuve had to go the long way round – outside. There he found no grip and went off on to the grass, bounced across that and came back on, but seventh.

Schumacher led.

Barrichello (Stewart) stalled on the grid, halting the race. Schumacher would have to do it again at the re-start and did, producing enough power to lead Villeneuve into the corkscrew. Villeneuve tracked him, applied power of his own as they crossed the line to complete the lap and went by. Soon enough Berger did the same and after the pit stops Schumacher

drifted back to fifth. Much ado about nothing.

Argentina became a cameo of what can go wrong. He qualified on the second row and into the first corner brushed against Barrichello, spinning the Stewart and ramming it. Frentzen's Williams was spewing oil, clutch problems; this smeared Schumacher's visor so he couldn't see. He was out.

Three races into the season Villeneuve led the Championship with 20 points, Schumacher fifth on 8. *Could* his abilities mask the superiority held by Williams and McLaren over a whole season? This was quite different from conjuring a win here and there by the astute application of tactics, or poaching a win if it rained. More poignantly, any assault on the Championship would need to acquire momentum soon or Villeneuve, Frentzen, Hakkinen and Coulthard would be too far away.

That increased the pressure at the **San Marino** Grand Prix. Qualifying offered moments of hope because he was fastest early on but Villeneuve took pole from Frentzen. Schumacher made another strong start in the race and, by clinging to Villeneuve, was past Frentzen who swarmed, could find no way through. These three front-runners settled to equidistance although there'd be move and countermove, advance and retreat to the first of two pit stops. These pit stops, between laps 23 and 26, were pivotal because they gave Frentzen the lead from Schumacher. Villeneuve, running third, suffered a gearbox failure on lap 41 just before the second stops. Frentzen pitted first and that might have allowed Schumacher one of his sprints but Nicola Larini (Sauber) balked him. Frentzen won.

'I was basically happy,' Schumacher said. 'Second position was [GRIMACE] more than I was expecting, I was expecting third. I hoped to get in between the Williamses, which finally happened. I could have done a little bit better before my second pit stop if I wouldn't have had this traffic issue with Larini who was suddenly driving very slowly. I locked up my front right tyre, flat-spotted it and I had to come in so I couldn't follow my plan' – the sprint.

Imola had altered the Championship significantly. Villeneuve was still on 20 of course but Schumacher was up to 14, with Coulthard, Berger, Hakkinen, Frentzen and Irvine grouped on 10.

The Ferrari was clearly moving towards the pace although it was not there yet. I asked Byrne how important it is to have somebody like Schumacher when you are going through the process of reaching that pace and rectifying faults.

Locking up a little in Australia, where he finished second to David Coulthard. (Formula One Pictures)

'Vital. That's one thing Michael is very good at, really knowing if you make a change to a car whether it's actually going to make it faster. All drivers are able to get the car balanced the way they want it but there is always the question mark *OK, it's well balanced but does it have more grip? Is it potentially faster?* I've found with Michael that if you give him a car with more grip he can normally find a way to drive it. If the car's got the grip, even if the balance is not right he adapts his style, finds a way. He has this ability to experiment with various lines round various corners depending on the car's handling and he is able to get the best out of the car even if the car's not 100 per cent. That's

unique. That's certainly not something all drivers have.'

Monaco offered possibilities, as it does to the driver who harnesses pace, precision and persistence. Among the mountain of Monaco clichés is one mouthed annually that pole position is decisive. It isn't. Frentzen (1m 18.216s) took that from Schumacher (1m 18.235s), with Villeneuve and Giancarlo Fisichella (Jordan) on the next row. 'I did three laps all around the same time,' Schumacher said, 'which just shows that we pulled the maximum out of the car. I tried again at the end but I couldn't improve. I just had too much understeer.'

Another Monaco cliché is that the

Mediterranean has azure blue skies coated with endless molten sunshine. Anyone who has been there regularly learns to pack waders, sou'westers and water wings. The weather is fickle. On Sunday 11 May the forecast reflected this, drizzle which would turn to rain half an hour before the start and then stop fairly soon after. It was horribly, horribly inconclusive to each team now facing the critical decision about what weather to prepare the car for.

Williams gambled that the forecasters were right and the rain would stop, so they set Frentzen and Villeneuve up for the dry. In the pit lane Schumacher hesitated, weighing the case for and against. He had one Ferrari set up as the Williamses were, the other (the spare car) a compromise – intermediate. The decision could not long be postponed because he had to bring the chosen car to the grid. The decision on tyres, however, could wait until he was there.

Todt watched carefully. 'Michael hesitated a great deal. Finally, 20 minutes before the start [five minutes before the pit lane closed] he alone took the decision and moved towards the car chassis number 175,' the intermediate.

Schumacher was circumspect, almost matter-of-fact. 'I decided to jump into that one at the last possible moment.'

On the grid he asked for more wing and selected intermediate tyres while at that moment Frentzen's car, alongside, was being fitted with dries. 'I was truly astonished,' Schumacher would say, 'and it perturbed me a bit.' He'd had the feeling that the track might 'dry quickly' but nothing here on the grid could prove that and he knew 'if I'd made a mistake' it would require an additional pit stop to change to the right tyres. That would be a dozen places gone.

The clarity of greatness: it's easier to drive on intermediate tyres in the dry than dry tyres in the wet and, looking at the track surface now, intermediates will give an instant advantage whatever happens afterwards.

Behind him Villeneuve's Williams was being fitted with dry tyres.

Stepney glimpsed Schumacher's face

and it glistened. Stepney knew exactly what that meant.

The cars moved away on the formation lap and somewhere the far side of Casino Square the rain hardened. Each of the 22 drivers knew their luck or their fate before they settled on the grid. When the red lights went off Frentzen felt his way forward and within perhaps 20 yards Schumacher had pulled ahead, long before Ste. Devote decisively ahead. He drew Fisichella, also on intermediates, through in his slipstream. By Ste. Devote he led Fisichella by some 30 yards, and Fisichella was already clear of both Williamses.

'Yes, I made a terrific start,' Fisichella says, 'especially considering that I had intermediate tyres and Michael had full rain tyres. That's why the Ferrari immediately took a big advantage but my thinking was only to do my best in these weather conditions. When you have to make pit stops, strategy is important and so normally you're thinking about your own race.' This is doubly interesting because Schumacher was as we know on intermediate tyres and would only switch to full wets at his sole pit stop (at the end of lap 32).

When you see a twinkle in the driver's eye you know he'll perform

At the top of the hill Schumacher had extended his lead although exiting Casino Square, where the track looked like grey ice, the Ferrari tugged and twitched. He caught that.

He approached the little dip towards the right for the tunnel, approached the place where the year before he'd butted the barrier so ignominiously. 'In attacking this zone of the circuit on that first lap I was super-prudent. And anyway, from Mirabeau to the tunnel during the whole race I'd be in big difficulties. On the one hand I had the impression I was going so slowly that I could have got out of the car and walked alongside it, on the other hand that I'd not backed off enough.'

Fisichella did close the gap a little but after the tunnel Schumacher restored it, no nonsense. Onto the start-finish straight – the wrenching right at Rascasse's culmination – the Ferrari tugged and twitched again, but that was from the power he was wringing from it. As he crossed the line *Fisichella was not yet in sight*.

The gap froze when eventually Fisichella did cross the line:

	Schumacher	Fisichella	Gain
Lap 1	1: 58.768	2: 05.442	+ 6.674

Nigel Stepney's reaction is revealing because it's how those closely involved think: not triumphalist, not clenched fist in the air, but feet firmly on the ground. 'You just hope the [expletive] thing's going to hang together …'

You can argue that Fisichella was young (24). He was only in his second season of grand prix racing, he had yet to score a single point, and however super-prudent Schumacher was, Fisichella would be more prudent still. This was *Monaco* and he was running *second*. You can argue that he had only driven one grand prix here before, in 1996 for Minardi, when he'd qualified eighteenth and crashed on the first lap. Now, amid all this grey-ice treachery and the Armco always so close, if Schumacher made any semblance of a mistake Fisichella might *win*.

Stepney casts a knowing gaze over Schumacher's achievement. 'Sometimes you see a twinkle in a driver's eye. Doesn't matter if, say, they've qualified third or fourth – well, it didn't matter so much before 1999 [when it's been much harder to gain places]. Take Michael. Might not go particularly well in the Sunday morning warm-up, doesn't matter, in the race he'll perform. You can see when he's ready to do that. He's cool and his eyes are glistening and he's *loaded* for the race. You can see he's loaded, see he's ready for it. Some you never see it in but with Senna you could too, and nine times out of ten they do something special when you do see it. They're all hyped up and *ready*. It's

This is what Schumacher sees, here pictured at Interlagos. (Formula One Pictures)

very difficult to read drivers but sometimes you can.'

To explore this opening lap further, here are the various states of disarray of the next four drivers to cross the line after Fisichella.

Ralf Schumacher	@ 8.512s
Frentzen	@ 8.717s
Barrichello	@ 9.938s
Johnny Herbert (Sauber)	@ 10.895s

Now listen to Fisichella. 'No, I wasn't intimidated by Schumacher's sudden disappearance [into the distance]. You have to consider many parameters that can change a car's performance, fuel on board, tyres and so on. We were expecting the weather to change a little and so, with the intermediate tyres, we would have had an advantage.

You assume that the man in front will brake there and then too

'If the weather stayed the same, as in fact it did, it was pointless to worry about the Ferrari. You mustn't forget that my car had a dry set-up, with a few changes made on the grid. Before the start Schumacher jumped out from his race car to the T-car prepared with a wet setting. My thinking was simply to do my best to reach the best possible place and to keep other drivers under pressure. I was not at all intimidated by being second. I've always been fighting for top places ever since I started racing, and I'd won the Monaco Formula 3 race in 1994 so I was cool and calm. If I did it in Formula 3 I can do it in Formula 1.'

The second lap heightened the feeling of disbelief. Schumacher circled in a dimension entirely his own. Rain still fell hard. He reached Mirabeau, which affords a view all the way back to Casino Square, and *Fisichella was not yet in sight*. By the end of this lap the gap had widened to 11 seconds.

	Schumacher	Fisichella	Gain
Lap 2	1: 54.747	1: 59.613	+ 4.866

He settled to a rhythm but it was between four and five seconds a lap faster than Fisichella so that, completing lap 3, the leader board had become a freak, as if two distinct events were being held simultaneously, Schumacher in one, the rest in the other.

Lap 3	1: 55.456	1: 59.654	+ 4.198

Translating that into overall gaps, this is the leader board which really was a freak.

Fisichella	@ 15.718s
Ralf Schumacher	@ 16.648s
Barrichello	@ 16.965s
Herbert	@ 18.614s
Olivier Panis (Prost)	@ 24.689s

Five cars had spun or crashed and they would not be the last.

Did it matter to Fisichella that Schumacher was literally out of sight?

'No. With different race strategies cars can be very 'different' at the starting line. You have to do your best, as you do in qualifying, but now do it between the pit stops, and only in the last part of the race can you directly face your opponents.'

How hard is it to drive Monaco in the wet? Herbert, who had been making such safe and steady progress, says: 'The actual track itself is not too bad. The problem is the white lines, so many white lines [the normal road markings]. Over the years they have tried to burn them off – they've tried to do the crossings – and that is the trickiest part. Sometimes when they've burnt them off they are still slippery. And that year it was quite bad.'

And visibility? 'Cars have rear lights, but you can't see them because there is so much spray and it is so dense. You see peripherally – you can see the Armco so you can see where you are, although not what's immediately in front if it's very, very wet.'

And braking? 'You know where you're going to brake' – and each driver works on the assumption that the man in front will be braking there and then too. But if something happens to him? 'Then you don't know.' You just steam into him?

Qualifying at Monaco was dry and sunny. (Formula One Pictures)

'Yes.' And you can't gauge your braking by listening to the engine noise of the car ahead? 'You can't because you can't hear it!'

Herbert pauses, evaluating Schumacher that day. 'It's much easier when you are in the lead and have a clear road, but he was pretty good. I think the drive he did in Barcelona was probably better.'

	Schumacher	Fisichella	Gain
Lap 4	1: 57.040	1: 58.070	+ 1.030
Lap 5	1: 54.308	1: 59.681	+ 5.373

On lap 5 the gap was a chasm at 22.121 seconds and, increasing the sense of disbelief, at this rate Schumacher would have lapped the entire field by lap 25, well under half distance. Barrichello held the inside line down to the harbour chicane and overtook Fisichella. What could he do about Schumacher? Anything? Nothing? Schumacher set fastest lap …

Ralf overtook Fisichella, two Schumachers in the first three.

Round Mirabeau the Ferrari lurched and floated towards the Armco but he rode that, didn't touch anything. At 9 laps he led Barrichello by 28.465 seconds, which in the physical dimension meant that as Barrichello broke the timing beam on the start-finish line Schumacher was already somewhere the other side of Casino Square. That did not completely obscure the fact that Barrichello was driving hard enough to match Schumacher.

	Schumacher	Barrichello	Gain/loss
Lap 9	1: 53.821	1: 54.225	+ 0.404
Lap 10	1: 53.788	1: 53.495	− 0.293
Lap 11	1: 54.564	1: 54.603	+ 0.039
Lap 12	1: 54.641	1: 57.059	+ 2.418

On lap 15 he lapped Villeneuve, who already carried punishment from the Armco. Completing that lap, when Barrichello broke the beam – the chasm now 30.436 – Schumacher was already at Mirabeau. Ralf Schumacher crashed and Fisichella ran third again but at 47.990 seconds, translating to nearly half a lap. On lap 17 Villeneuve retired, so that Schumacher would lead the

Championship if he won. He pitted on lap 31 with the comfort of 41 seconds in hand and changed to full wets, the rain falling harder.

They'd stop the race after two hours, or 62 laps of the original 78, and he had but a single instant of alarm on the journey to that point.

'During the whole race,' he'd say, 'I had trouble braking. At Ste. Devote I was often locking my front wheels.'

The clarity of greatness: one of these laps I might get into trouble there – I mustn't let that take me by surprise if it should happen.

On lap 53 'I couldn't slow down enough' at Ste. Devote.

Without doubt I can take the corner but I risk hitting the Armco on the exit. I'll go straight on into the safe embrace of the escape road, I'll do a U-turn and I'll return unmolested.

'There was no problem.'

The escape from the escape road was beautifully executed. He angled the Ferrari to go round Ste. Devote in the orthodox way, aborted it completely, slowed before the barrier at the end of the escape road, braked nicely, spun the car and continued undisturbed. The time-loss is reflected in lap times.

Lap 52	1: 54.325
Lap 53	2: 04.772
Lap 54	1: 55.420

He beat Barrichello by 53.306 seconds, the chasm maintained to the end, and did lead the Championship by four points from Villeneuve. He'd concede that, taking everything into consideration, it was a great win although a moment later he moderated that to 'an important one.' The moderation made you wonder what standards he was judging himself by. He made a neat little joke too. When someone asked him about Ste. Devote he said he'd seen a sea of Ferrari supporters waving their Prancing Horse flags and thought he'd give them a thrill. That apart, the race was 'mostly under control'.

I asked Stepney which was his favourite Schumacher race. 'Monte Carlo the year it was wet. That's personal, but to beat Monte Carlo is the best. Spain in the wet in '96 was fantastic but I just like to win at Monte Carlo. It's a place you have to go to, have to win and then get out. To do that gives me satisfaction.'

Rory Byrne was amazed to discover that the Ferrari mythology about winning was true. 'Here at Maranello on a Sunday night after Ferrari have won, they have to have extra police out controlling the traffic, the church bells are tolling. The place just goes crazy. They're honking their horns and waving Ferrari flags. On a Sunday night after a race win, wherever I go I never have to pay for a meal. They refuse to accept any money.

'It's a totally different sort of atmosphere to England, amazingly different. The first win after I arrived was Monaco and I could not believe it. Incredible! I hadn't imagined anything like that would happen. These people are passionate about it. The Fiorano circuit is quite close to apartments and so on. Rather than complain about the noise – and we test sometimes up to 9 o'clock at night in the summer – they are hanging out of the windows. They've got friends coming round, hanging off the balconies having a look! There'll be a traffic jam outside. There's a bridge going over a through-road and the bridge is jam-packed full of people looking at the circuit. Yes, amazing.'

Spain was the obverse of Monaco. Schumacher qualified on the fourth row and finished the race fourth nearly 18 seconds behind Villeneuve who took the Championship lead back. At the start Schumacher adopted the logical tactic at a place so friendly to the Williamses: make gains immediately. He used his reflexes to be on the power instantaneously and fled at an angle towards the inside line for the first corner, which he took in third place. He hunted down Coulthard and overtook on the outside but couldn't sustain this pace.

In **Canada** he had a taut pole from Villeneuve (1m 18.095 against 1m 18.108, which is 0.013 of a second). As Rory Byrne says, 'by Canada time we were on the pace.'

He made the better start and at the end of the first lap led Villeneuve by 1.472 seconds, something rendered irrelevant because Villeneuve hit the wall opposite the pits. Fisichella took up the chase. Schumacher, carrying a light fuel load, was on a three-stop strategy, Fisichella on two, so Schumacher had to gain the equivalent of a pit stop. The safety car was out after Ukyo Katayama (Minardi) crashed on lap 6, and that enabled Fisichella to draw up as the concertina closed behind the safety car. Schumacher had to gain the pit stop again and, the safety car gone, tried but Fisichella hung on and at 13 laps lay only 1.470 seconds behind.

Eventually Schumacher's hammer-hammer-hammering propelled him clear but after the pit stop scramble Coulthard led: he hadn't stopped. For the core of the race it was a tale of these two men, Coulthard maintaining the lead to lap 39 when he did stop, Schumacher leading to lap 43 (his second stop), Coulthard leading to lap 51 and *his*

> **The sky darkened, umbrellas went up and it began to rain**

second stop. Coulthard's clutch misbehaved and that passed the lead back to Schumacher, then Panis crashed heavily. The safety car came out again and this time escorted the ten cars who were still running round to the finishing line, no overtaking permitted. Schumacher 37 points, Villeneuve 30.

He said you took no pleasure from winning a race where somebody had been injured and, as chairman of the Drivers' Association, spoke about safety and how it is always under review, how the drivers discuss circuits after the races, how measures put in place were working 'not too badly.' The injuries to Panis, he concluded, could have been worse but 'we will continue to look at safety.' The dangers diminish but remain a constant.

Now the pressure twisted onto Villeneuve. In **France** that heightened because Schumacher took pole from Frentzen and brother Ralf – a fully

Germanic grid the like of which had never been seen before – Villeneuve fourth. That shaped the race, Schumacher, Frentzen, Irvine up to third, Villeneuve fourth. The order solidified although within that Schumacher smoothed the Ferrari through Magny-Cours' sweepers and constructed a gap of 4.161 seconds by lap 5, Villeneuve far adrift at 8.535s and still fourth. The pit stops? Schumacher was on two but so was Frentzen; Irvine and Villeneuve were both on three. Schumacher was travelling at such a pace early on, however, that Frentzen assumed he was carrying a light fuel load and it must be a three.

The clarity of greatness: he'd had a lot of trouble with the left front tyre in practice – Magny-Cours mostly right-handers throwing the weight onto the left going round them. So you modify your lines through the quick right-handers. It worked so effectively that he was surprised at 'how I could keep the left front alive.'

The leaders pitted at third distance and resumed, the order re-solidifying. The sky was darkening, and a regular visitor to Magny-Cours soon learns to pack the waders they took to Monaco. Schumacher accelerated to build a big gap against whatever the rain might bring.

	Schumacher	Frentzen	Gain/loss
Lap 34	1: 19.435	1: 18.786	– 0.649
Lap 35	1: 18.401	1: 18.580	+ 0.179
Lap 36	1: 18.117	1: 19.032	+ 0.915
Lap 37	1: 17.910	1: 20.483	+ 2.573
Lap 38	1: 17.926	1: 21.253	+ 3.327

At 40 laps, the gap up to 21.931 seconds, Schumacher was pressing on so urgently that he locked a tyre at one corner. He knew that from this urgency would come a lead giving him the option of stopping for wets if he wanted – and he'd still have the lead.

The sky darkened, umbrellas went up, and when Irvine pitted on lap 44 rain fell. Dark, bruised clouds seeped from the east

The race wasn't dry and sunny though. Schumacher makes an extraordinary start, Giancarlo Fisichella behind but already a long way back and the Williamses all at sea. (Formula One Pictures)

78

in a great arc. Schumacher pitted on lap 46 but for more dry tyres, the rain not yet heavy enough. That was exercising the option because everyone was making stops – Frentzen two laps later (dries) and Villeneuve on lap 52 (dries, too) – so they all lost roughly the same chunks of time but of course Schumacher had the equivalent of a pit stop in hand. Still the urgency held him and he extended the lead to 28.365.

	Schumacher	Frentzen	Gain
Lap 52	1:19.083	1: 19.233	+ 0.150
Lap 53	1:19.626	1: 21.572	+ 1.946
Lap 54	1:19.107	1: 23.660	+ 4.553
Lap 55	1:19.368	1: 20.063	+ 0.695

On lap 62 the rain fell hard and Schumacher went wide at the first corner, put two wheels onto the gravel, then all four, but kept the car moving and rejoined. He didn't pit and neither did Frentzen. Seven laps remained and he navigated them safely enough, beating Frentzen by 23.537 seconds, Villeneuve fourth, to lead the Championship with 47 points, Villeneuve 33.

Silverstone was straightforward, a Villeneuve win from pole, although at one point Schumacher led. A wheel bearing failed on lap 39. Schumacher 47, Villeneuve 43.

The **German** Grand Prix confused everything. From pole, Berger in the Benetton led from Fisichella, Schumacher third and running the second half of the race without fifth gear. He adapted to cope, Fisichella had a puncture and he was second. Berger won it by more than 17 seconds but Schumacher wasn't concerned about that. He wanted to know where Villeneuve had finished and was told he'd spun out on lap 34. Schumacher 53, Villeneuve 43.

In **Hungary** he had pole but his tyres blistered during the race and he limped to fourth. Worse, Hill ought to have won but a throttle problem near the end let Villeneuve in. Schumacher 56, Villeneuve 53.

Six races remained. If you're going to **Belgium** don't forget the waders because although Spa is much shorter than in the old days it's still 4.3 miles (6.9 kilometres) and, truly, it can be summer at La Source, autumn at Les Combes, winter at Fagnes and springtime at Stavelot all on the same lap. This is Schumacher country, and not just because it's close to Kerpen and well stocked by Germans over the race weekend. It's Schumacher country because great drivers exploit those four seasons.

Trevor Foster, with Jordan when that team gave Schumacher his debut at Spa in 1991, amplifies the point and, yes, it really is stunningly simple. 'The great ones go to every race asking themselves a single question: how can I win here? They don't say, if only I had a Williams or whatever, don't say if only things were like this or like that. They say: this is what I have, now where can I find an edge? And they look everywhere for it.' (Schumacher sat on the grid – the fourth row – with Nelson Piquet on the row in front and Piquet had driven more grands prix than Schumacher had driven laps. Foster had no doubts about what Schumacher was thinking. *I am going to win here*.)

He'd been 23 then, was 29 now. He'd grown into a man, still rangy, still angular but capable of maintaining rarest harmony amid the sudden-shifting currents of a race.

He qualified third, behind Villeneuve and Alesi, and that in the spare car. He wrung the fast lap out of himself – three quarters of the way through the session he'd been down in seventh – and murmured about how much work needed to be done.

Twenty minutes before the start of the race it rained. He reasoned that he needed as much information as possible before deciding which car to choose. His race car was set up for the dry and the spare was a compromise with intermediate tyres and a lighter fuel load – and that would allow

Victory, with Rubens Barrichello looking delighted too, Jean Todt beaming and Irvine knackered! (Formula One Pictures)

him to gain enough time to make an early pit stop for dry tyres, if that was necessary.

He went out and did a reconnaissance lap in the race car searching, monitoring, weighing, projecting.

Too much water.

He made his decision to race the spare, leaving the decision so late that he was the final car to arrive on the grid. He looked around. Almost everybody else was on wet

tyres. He thought that if this was only a shower, then when it passed the intermediate tyres would be a good thing to have and the others would be crippled on full wets.

Schumacher got lucky because the track was awash and the race would begin behind the safety car. Now, on the grid, Schumacher got luckier still. He glimpsed sun emerging from the clouds.

They skated and shivered three laps shrouded in spray and when the safety car released them Villeneuve set off with Alesi somewhere in the waterfall behind, and Schumacher close to Alesi. Out of Les Combes Schumacher tried the inside but Alesi was having none of that. The onboard camera caught Schumacher's skill because Alesi's rear tyres spewed spray but from within that Schumacher con-

trived the attack. At the entry to the Bus Stop he feinted inside but Alesi was having none of that either. Towards La Source hairpin they slithered in tandem across the standing water and Schumacher did take the inside, Alesi seeming to be turning across; didn't.

Villeneuve was 1.545 seconds ahead.

By Les Combes Schumacher had caught him and stole a glance down the inside but wasn't close enough. At Rivage, the right horseshoe after Les Combes, he did go inside and floated past Villeneuve in something approaching regal splendour, drew away. Villeneuve would not see him again. At lap 5 he led by 5.873 seconds and next lap Villeneuve pitted for intermediates. Schumacher had gone ten seconds faster than anyone else on that lap.

At lap 6

| Schumacher | 2: 08.743 |
| Fisichella | 2: 18.454 |

At lap 9 he led Fisichella by 34 seconds and soon that would be 47. The way it was developing he'd have enough time to nip back to Kerpen, take afternoon tea, motor back and still be in the lead.

	Schumacher	*Fisichella*	*Gain*
Lap 9	2: 06.578	2: 12.784	+ 6.206
Lap 10	2: 05.781	Pit	
Lap 11	2: 06.204	2: 33.123	After pit stop
Lap 12	2: 05.226	2: 11.239	+ 6.013

Significantly Salo, who'd been on full wets, changed to dries and on lap 12 set fastest lap.

	Schumacher	*Salo*	*Loss*
Lap 13	2: 09.121	2: 03.973	– 5.148

Schumacher pitted for dries on lap 14, was stationary for 8.0 seconds and rejoined. A dry line had formed. He led by 41 seconds, now from Alesi, but Alesi would have handling problems and Fisichella resumed in second place at 55.542 seconds. Schumacher made a second stop at his leisure later on, eased off and won by 'only' 26.753 seconds from Fisichella (Villeneuve fifth). Schumacher 66, Villeneuve 55.

He described the result as 'satisfactory' which, even as understatements go, is going a bit. Nor was it just that he'd sought out and maximised an advantage. This moderation – *satisfactory* – made you wonder again about the standard he was judging himself by. He added sternly that everybody knows how fast things can change. He might have been previewing the **Italian** Grand Prix at Monza.

There the Ferrari was off the pace (Villeneuve fifth, he sixth) and off the pace in **Austria,** compounded by a stop-go penalty when he overtook Frentzen under yellow flags. Villeneuve won: Schumacher, sixth again, 68, Villeneuve 67, three races left.

He qualified fifth for the **Luxembourg** Grand Prix at the Nürburgring but the distance from the grid to the first corner, a right-hander, is long enough for places to be won and lost; and the first corner enjoys a specific notoriety. It can throttle a column of advancing cars.

When the red lights went off the McLarens and Williamses moved clear. Initially Schumacher moved over to the right so that he had Fisichella outside him but Ralf drew up outside Fisichella and went past. Schumacher immediately darted away to the left, Ralf and Fisichella travelling abreast towards the corner. Ralf turned in, squeezing Fisichella so hard he put two wheels on the grass; and Schumacher, now himself abreast of Ralf, turned in too. Fisichella tapped Ralf's rear and the Jordan was airborne, its right rear wheel passing very close to the Ferrari's cockpit.

This was the meeting in the most direct way.

Schumacher ploughed across the gravel run-off area and continued to the second lap when he pitted and stepped from the Ferrari. The car's handling felt strange, he'd say, so strange it caused him to run across the rumble-strip kerbing at the chicane. Hence the retirement.

He seemed to be stretching filial piety to its limits when he said 'it's a shame that the incident happened with my brother' but he did expand. 'I don't think anyone is to blame because it was not a deliberate move.' Villeneuve won and led 77–68.

Clearly Schumacher needed to win **Japan**. Although Villeneuve had pole (from him) Villeneuve was racing into great uncertainty because he'd ignored a yellow flag in the Saturday morning session, his fourth similar offence of the season, and been excluded from the race, then allowed in under appeal. Whatever points he earned might, and almost certainly would, be subsequently taken from him.

Villeneuve decided on an obvious tactic, to lead the race slowly hoping Schumacher would become embroiled in a jostling of the bunch which going slowly would create.

The clarity of greatness: we know what Villeneuve will almost certainly do and we must be prepared with a counter-tactic. Eddie will take on Villeneuve while Michael watches from a safe distance – and if we need to get Eddie past Michael to get at Villeneuve, let's decide now where on the circuit he'll do it. The curving right-hander? Yes, there.

After the red lights Villeneuve chopped in front of Schumacher blocking him and, when Schumacher tried to loop round the outside, Villeneuve threatened a nudge, forcing him back. Irvine ran fourth behind Hakkinen. Completing the opening lap Villeneuve had created the bunch because Berger, sixth, was only just over two seconds behind and that's a small span. On the second lap, approaching the curving right-hander, Irvine went past Hakkinen on the outside and stayed outside, moving past Schumacher too. If you didn't know, this looked like one of the great overtaking moves. If you did know, it looked like the consummation of the thinking team. Irvine caught Villeneuve apace, rasped out fastest lap and jinked past at the chicane.

This was uncomfortable for Villeneuve who knew that at some point Irvine would obey team orders and aid Schumacher.

The pit stops shook it up, although during them Schumacher gained enough to be present and correct when Villeneuve emerged from his, and Villeneuve made a muscular move across the track. What Villeneuve did, Schumacher said, 'could have been very dangerous.' Irvine slowed and let Schumacher through then held Villeneuve back; Villeneuve pitted again but the refuelling rig malfunctioned and he finished fifth. The Schumacher win set up the finale in the **European** Grand Prix at Jerez exquisitely.

Leaving Suzuka, Villeneuve had 79 points and Schumacher 78 but the FIA, the sport's governing body, maintained the ban, stripping Villeneuve of the two points for fifth. Williams did not appeal for fear the FIA might turn prickly and ban Villeneuve from Jerez. The new total, Schumacher leading 78–77, did not disturb the merciful simplicity of what would be happening amid the rolling, barren hills of Andalucia: whichever finished in front of the other was World Champion. If Villeneuve was third, fourth or fifth and Schumacher a place behind, they tied on points but Villeneuve took the tie-break on most wins over the season.

To have no difference between the 3 fastest laps was unknown

Grand prix racing had not been to Jerez, a tight sort of circuit in the modern way demanding patience and accuracy, for three years. This interval meant that the track lacked the grip you get when rubber is regularly burnished from Formula 1 car tyres, laying a film of adhesion; and also meant that the Friday times carried dubious overall significance. (Panis was quickest in the Prost, then Hill, Villeneuve third, Schumacher ninth.)

The Saturday morning practice session brought tension and temperament to the surface for the first time. Villeneuve made his way to Irvine, still sitting in the Ferrari, and berated him for balking. Waving his finger and stooping over the cockpit Villeneuve told Irvine to stop behaving like an idiot. This was, Villeneuve claimed, the fourth time so far during the meeting that Irvine had slowed and waited for him. 'We all know he is a clown,' Villeneuve said. Later Irvine riposted that Villeneuve always talked like that and what's the fuss?

The qualifying was like none Formula 1 had ever seen.

Villeneuve did a lap of 1m 21.072s.

Schumacher booted the Ferrari through the spoon of a left onto the finishing straight – the impetus hauling it

Prayers for a Schumacher victory were said in the old ornate church

onto the blue-white kerbing at the track's rim – and smoothed it to face directly ahead, forced it to the line. The timing devices froze at 1m 21.072s. To have no difference, to three decimal points, between the two fastest drivers was unknown.

Villeneuve tried to respond but went briefly onto the grass, wrecking the lap.

With ten minutes left Frentzen was booting the Williams into and out of the spoon, forcing it to the line. 1m 21.072s.

It brought the broadest smile from Schumacher.

The grid order was decided by *when* these three laps had been done, giving pole to Villeneuve, then Schumacher, then Frentzen. Irvine, seventh, accepted there wasn't much he could do to help Schumacher who had a Williams in front and a Williams behind.

The clarity of greatness: everything turns on the start because a good one gives me the lead into the first corner and I can win from there. I'll be lining up at the head of the right-hand column and the track is clean there. I watched for that at the start of the Formula 3000 race, and being on the right didn't seem to make a big difference.

The weather for the Sunday morning warm-up was cool and overcast. The cars waited obediently, strung down the pit lane, for the session to begin. These are moments of unstated, and sometimes disguised, tension because what happens here can have a direct bearing on the race. Hakkinen went quickest, Villeneuve fifth, Schumacher seventh. The talk fell to sub-lots: Schumacher had three new sets of

tyres left from his allocation, Villeneuve and Frentzen only two so they'd start on old ones. An edge for Schumacher?

In Kerpen the Schumacher indoor kart track had been converted into a cinema and 800 guests, sitting on moulded blue plastic chairs in mini-grandstands, would watch the race. The solid burgers of the town itself prepared with their habitual self-control, hanging Prancing Horse flags beside their window boxes. In the square a pretty lady sold hats and tee-shirts from a trestle table while, nearby, young men who'd already bought the tee-shirts wheeled beer kegs away on trolleys. A little girl wore a Ferrari scarf and *Schumi* was painted on her face in mum's lipstick. A man banged a big base drum which had a clown's face etched on it. A man had trimmed a bush in a giant pot to look like a Ferrari.

German television was carrying pictures of Willi Weber showing off *Michael Schumacher 1997 F1 World Champion* tee-shirts, which might have been tempting fate even if you don't believe in things like that.

In the square at Maranello autumnal sunlight cast long, precise shadows from the people who already waited. They'd grow to 10,000, watching the race on a giant screen. Prayers for a Schumacher victory were said in the old, ornate church, its spires pointing to heaven like fragile stalagmites. The flowers in the windowboxes at the town hall were Ferrari red and from the upper windows of houses hung the Prancing Horse flags, just like in Kerpen.

Two communities, so different in many ways, had found communion.

Jody Scheckter was at Jerez bearing his open and slightly quizzical smile as he moved about. He had the businessman's haircut, its shape and length conventionally modest. The years had touched him, but lightly. Did he remember in living detail that sun-dappled late afternoon when Gilles Villeneuve followed him out of Parabolica and the stands rose and the world was his, all his? Had he come to be dispossessed, and what did he think of that? The years had touched his South African accent, softening it perhaps, but the thinking remained the same: in motor racing you take what you get. If he'd remain the last Ferrari driver to win it, OK. If Schumacher now took that from him, OK.

Scheckter could do nothing except watch, just like everybody else.

Autumn sunlight fell across Jerez, warm enough for Schumacher to peel off his overalls down to his white tee-shirt on the short journey from the pits to the transporter. The tee-shirt was decorated with Ferrari and Marlboro logos but nothing about being Champion 1997. He looked as he always did approaching pressure, perfectly composed.

Brawn, standing somewhere near the Ferrari pit, smiled in his benevolent schoolmasterly way. 'Everything seemed fine in the warm-up. No problems. We're just getting ready for the race now,' he'd say, quick and clipped, revealing absolutely nothing.

What strategy do you think Williams will have? someone wanted to know. You might as well ask the Pentagon for atomic formulae. Brawn's smile broadened to a great big grin – 'I don't know' – and he was gone into the shadows of the pit.

At the kart track at Kerpen the German television channel *RTL* interviewed Rolf and Elisabeth. She was small, straw-blonde, and wore a yellow anorak. Curious. You could not see the lineage in her face or eyes. She masticated what appeared to be chewing gum absently, mechanically, perhaps as an aid to calming herself.

The combatants have been asked how they prepared for the great day. How do you as parents feel about it?

'I do not prepare myself and I am worried,' she said.

What time did you get up?

'Half past six.'

Had a coffee?

'Yes.'

Do you talk to Frentzen's mother or Villeneuve's mother?

'No, I don't do that. I don't know them. I have no contact.'

Formula 1 always attracts admirers from showbusiness. Schumacher with Phil Collins and his wife. (Formula One Pictures)

Rolf wore a hip-length coat and a blue shirt. He had white, receding, dignified hair and spectacles. Curious. The lineage to Michael was uncannily evident in his face, the set of his eyes, the curl of his mouth. 'It appears I am very composed but as a father you get quite wound up. First of all I want to wish every driver in the race good luck.' He pointed out that whatever happened Michael would be 'deputy' World Champion. 'There are a lot of drivers who never made it that far …'

Allegedly you gave him lessons in driving using lamp posts?

Rolf then recounted the story of the four-year-old Schumacher who was told not to go too fast and of course did.

The parents weren't unduly defensive and certainly not demonstrative, just caught up in something they could influence no more than Scheckter could, ordinary people expressing themselves as ordinary people do.

On the grid a melee pressed closer and closer to Villeneuve's car, so dense that he and the car vanished within it.

Brawn stood beside Schumacher's Ferrari, minder of the munitions.

The width of the track was a scuffling spread of guests, mechanics, officials and media all playing human skittles as they gathered and dispersed and gathered again, peering, posing, working, trying to work.

Somewhere over there was Hill's Arrows, in the bay on the grid behind Schumacher and next to Frentzen. That had become another sub-plot. Schumacher said plaintively that he considered Hill the third Williams driver and 'I hope he stays out of the way.' As they say in Scottish football, retaliate first just in case.

Scheckter was interviewed on this grid, the melee ebbing by, and explained that if Schumacher won then Italy would go wild. He added that when you drive for Ferrari you represent the Italian nation.

Maximum effort in Germany. (Formula One Pictures)

The grid cleared quickly, as it is does. The 22 cars moved off into the formation lap, Villeneuve drawing them round slowly, taking his place to the left of the grid, Schumacher to the right. They faced 69 laps, slightly under 190 miles (305.5 kilometres).

Five red lights – off.

Villeneuve came over to mid-track but Schumacher had made a fine start, clean and swift, and taken the lead. Frentzen was past Villeneuve. Crossing the line to complete the opening lap, Frentzen was at 1.981 seconds and Villeneuve at 3.221 from Schumacher and it settled like that

until Frentzen let Villeneuve through on lap 8. The first crisis of the race was at hand. Could Villeneuve catch Schumacher, 4.3 seconds ahead? At lap 9 he'd reduced it by a fraction to 4.256 seconds. He pushed hard enough to set fastest laps but Schumacher responded, setting fastest laps too.

	Schumacher	Villeneuve	Gain/loss
Lap 10	1: 24.521	1: 24.310	− 0.211
Lap 11	1: 24.514	1: 24.554	+ 0.040
Lap 12	1: 24.256	1: 24.950	+ 0.694

At lap 11 the overall gap between them was 4.085, and this is how it moved: at lap 13, 4.889; at lap 18, 5.144; at lap 20, 5.237 seconds.

They ran towards the first pits stops, Schumacher making his on lap 22, Villeneuve on lap 23 and this revised the order to Frentzen, Hakkinen, Schumacher, Coulthard, Villeneuve. Frentzen cut his pace by two seconds a lap, creating a bunch: Hakkinen drew up to him, Schumacher to Hakkinen, Coulthard to Schumacher. Villeneuve set a new fastest lap and drew up to Coulthard. When Frentzen, Hakkinen and Coulthard pitted, as they would soon, Villeneuve could attack Schumacher. By

lap 28 those pit stops had been completed, Schumacher back in the lead, Villeneuve back in second place. The second crisis of the race was at hand. Could Villeneuve mount the attack? He nibbled into the corner called Dry Sack, a spoon-shaped right, withdrew. That was the opening salvo.

	Schumacher	Villeneuve	Gain/loss	Overall
Lap 28	1: 25.331	1: 25.902	+ 0.571	1.056
Lap 29	1: 24.701	1: 24.594	– 0.107	0.950
Lap 30	1: 25.663	1: 25.536	– 0.127	0.822

The new tyres were helping Villeneuve just as the used ones had hindered him across the first stint.

They reached Norberto Fontana in the Sauber at the Ayrton Senna chicane with its a sharp right entry, and Fontana moved clear to give Schumacher right of passage, moved back and impeded Villeneuve. Cryptically Villeneuve would point out that Sauber used Ferrari engines.

At lap 31 the gap was 3.186. Villeneuve, dogged as a terrier, set about drawing up again and by lap 34 had it down to 2.343. He pushed harder and two laps later had it under two seconds, then under a second and a half. At lap 39 it was 1.041.

They weaved paths through back-markers and ran tight to the second pit stops, Schumacher's on lap 43 (stationary for 9.4 seconds and enough fuel to go to the end), Villeneuve's a lap later (8.3 seconds, and enough fuel too). Villeneuve emerged behind Coulthard and, maddeningly, couldn't get past him. Instant by instant Schumacher escaped. It was only a lap before Coulthard pitted – but a long lap and, when he did, the gap had opened to 2.590. Villeneuve knew that tyre wear would become critical very soon: too worn to mount the attack. He estimated he had three laps to catch and despatch Schumacher or the Championship was gone.

	Schumacher	Villeneuve	Gain/loss
Lap 46	1: 25.657	1: 24.093	– 1.564
Lap 47	1: 25.966	1: 25.325	– 0.641

It meant 1.026 separated them, nothing really. Villeneuve pummelled the gap again to catch Schumacher and they came across the line to start lap 48 separated by 0.385 of a second, in real terms less than nothing.

Villeneuve hustled him through and out of Expo 92, the right at the end of the pit lane straight, tracked him through Michelin, another right, tracked him on through the next left, closed up through the long, elegant right-hander after that. They travelled in lock-step down the descending straight to the right-twisting spoon of Dry Sack.

They were positioned over to the left, a ribbon of blue and white kerb coursing by at their elbows.

Villeneuve jinked right into the expanse of empty track, Schumacher level but outside him.

At the entry to the corner Villeneuve was nicely on the inside, Schumacher crowding him hard.

Villeneuve was half a car's length ahead but, with Schumacher to his left and the grass to his right, he had nowhere to go except ahead. The crowding was so hard that momentarily he put two wheels on the grass.

With shocking suddenness the Ferrari turned into him, its right-front wheel smacking the bodywork of the Williams beside the cockpit.

Villeneuve 'wasn't really surprised when he finally decided to turn in on me. It was a little bit expected so I knew I was taking a big risk [in trying to overtake].'

The Ferrari dribbled off into the gravel trap on the left but Villeneuve drove on, amazed that the car appeared to be undamaged after the strength of the hit it had just taken. Schumacher sat beached on the gravel, his rear wheels spinning but finding no propulsion. He clambered out and marched away, hauled his crash helmet off and stood on a low wall watching Villeneuve go by, Villeneuve go by.

The crash looked damning enough for Schumacher from a distance, but his on-board camera compounded that mercilessly. When the tape of it was played moments later every televiewer in the world could watch Villeneuve there on the inside, Schumacher crowding, then Schumacher's gloved hands twisting the steering wheel so that the Ferrari rammed the Williams. This was impossible to miss.

Someone on a scooter gave Schumacher a lift back to the pits while Villeneuve went by, Villeneuve went by to win the title. It didn't matter that at the very end he ceded the lead to Hakkinen and second place to Coulthard. Third was sufficient now and Jody Scheckter was still the last Ferrari Champion.

The fallout reverberated.

Schumacher claimed Villeneuve's over-taking move was 'optimistic' and 'I was very surprised by what he did'. But this was an extremely optimistic defence and ultimately untenable. At a Press Conference days later at Maranello Schumacher softened his stance, conceding that 'I made an error' and adding 'I'm a human, not a machine.'

Two weeks after Jerez the FIA's World Motor Sports Council ruled that he be stripped of his second place in the Championship but nothing more except the penance of doing a week's public relations on road safety for the European Commission. Max Mosley, President of the FIA, explained that the Council felt Schumacher's move was not pre-meditated but an instinctive action.

Schumacher revealed that he hadn't slept properly for three nights after the race 'because of the pressure I felt for what I had done. It was an instinctive action and it was important they decided it was not deliberate.'

The crash raised questions about the level of desire Schumacher worked to, and whether, if you are to win consistently in motor racing at its peak, you have to find defeat intolerable. Sportsmanship in any recognisable sense had been sacrificed a decade before, on the alter of Senna who crashed Prost twice in similar circumstances. But hadn't Villeneuve just proved you can win and conduct yourself decently? Wouldn't Hakkinen move from this first grand prix win of his career to the 1998 and then the 1999 Championships exhibiting the most becoming conduct?

The Jerez crash left other questions unanswered. Did the strength of the modern car allow drivers to take risks which could well have been fatal a generation before? Did the people who invest in grand prix racing for its television ratings *delight* in the crash and the fallout – nobody injured, and wonderful for the viewing figures? Did the FIA duck its responsibility by slapping Schumacher so limply on the wrist rather than kicking his backside all the way back up the autobahns to Kerpen?

Jerez was a mess of human weaknesses, Schumacher's the most visible, the catalyst.

Barnard was long gone from Ferrari but I was curious about his evaluation of Schumacher's strengths, about what Schumacher has that made good judges place him in with Fangio and Moss and Clark and Senna.

They have an extra capacity – and classic mind-blowing concentration

'How do you explain it? If you look at those top-top guys, and I'm talking about the Prosts and Laudas [as well], they have a dedication which the others don't understand. They have such a total immersion in what they are doing and an exclusion of everything else.

'They all have a natural skill at driving a racing car and that's second nature – going quickly is second nature. That leaves them a lot of capacity while they are driving to think about the car and the tyres and so on. *Where do I need it better? How do I make it better? I'll talk about this with my engineer,* and so on and so on. It's what they are all able to do, and they have this classic, mind-blowing dedication. It can grind the engineers into dust. Senna? I've known the technical people say "I can't keep up with him, I just can't keep up with him." They are so *into it* all the time.

'Schumacher was very similar, although perhaps less on the car side [demanding to know every detail about the car] and more on the total dedication side, the whole keep fit thing. He's going to be fit-

The very controversial crash at Jerez which decided the Championship in favour of Jacques Villeneuve: the cars in contact … Schumacher beached … and facing the consequences. (LAT)

ter than the next guy, he's going to be the fittest guy, he will make *sure* he's the fittest guy. Then he's going to have more of what he thinks are the right people round him to make *sure* he's going to do the job better. He's going to take everything one step more.'

I was curious, too, about Barnard's view on the strategy of mid-race sprints which Schumacher creates to order, particularly as the driver already seems to be going as fast as he can.

'The important part of the question is *going as fast as they can.* Sometimes you know for an absolute fact that they are not. It happens time and time again: somebody "falls off," there's a sniff of points or something and *bomp*, suddenly the stopwatch is going faster. You're asking about the driver "what have you been doing up to now?" It's all about motivation. The good ones are still motivated even when they are sitting on the back of the grid. They think: "OK, I know I am back here but I am going to do *this*, I am going to do *that* and I know I can get up there." The other guys are out there just going round and round – and there's a lot of them doing it.

'Everybody talks about good strategies and marvellous strategies, and it's all very well being aware of what you need to do, all very well going on the radio and saying *you have so many laps to gain so many seconds* but [CHUCKLE] it's no good saying that to the guy who can't do it! If you'd said something like that to Berger he'd have told you to eff off because he's going as hard as he can. Some of them would take a very dim view of being told to go faster and they'd think you were being [expletive] rude with "do you mind going quicker now?" Schumacher doesn't gear up to do a quick racing lap, he goes *over* his racing lap. Again it's dedicated concentration, the ability to switch everything else off and keep a focus on this one thing.'

Some drivers are sweaty after a race. Others – especially Schumacher – look almost fresh.

'That's the difference between the naturally talented guys and the guys who want it so badly and push themselves to do it. That's what Mansell was. For many, many years he wasn't considered to be worthwhile at all, but they come to a point – Hunt was the same, Hunt had one year – where they feel that they've either got a car that can do it or they've got a team behind them that is big enough to allow them to do it. Whatever it is, they think the situation is good enough and they won't get too many chances like this again.

'They decide inwardly, in their own minds, *this is my chance, I have to do it now, I am going to drive over my limit to do it.* And that's what Mansell did. I saw him drive absolute blinders in qualifying and it was only because he's got enormous balls – and enormous balls are part of the determination built on *this is my chance, if I don't take it now forget it, I'm never going to do it at all.* Tremendous driver, old Nigel. He said to me on many occasions "you get the car close enough, I'll fix the rest of it." He'd get in and big balls it round.'

Barnard pauses, reflects, points out that Hunt was a 'one-time Champion whereas Schumacher, Senna, Prost, they say "ah, so that's how you win a Championship" and they win more. That's the difference.'

Barnard pauses again.

'With Schumacher, the fundamental driving talent is there, the quickness, the reactions, the balls – it's all there. He's just bloody quick and all the good ones are that, just bloody quick. On to the top of that you can then pile all the baggage of peripherals, all the problems they have to deal with outside the car. The good ones kick that part into gear as well. Then you've got it.'

chapter four

Stalled (1998)

The F300 was launched in early January amid the habitual pomp, but Ross Brawn put a hard blade into that: 'This year only total success will be good enough.' Luca di Montezemolo put his own blade in too. 'Today is the first time we can say with belief that Ferrari can win the World Championship. We start the season absolutely aware that our objective is to win it.'

Schumacher tested the car at Fiorano and Jerez and had problems with, among other things, the gearbox electronics. He covered only 33 laps in two days. He tested at Mugello and described the car as having 'that certain kind of nervousness that a racing car should have.' Hakkinen in the new McLaren had broken the winter testing record at Barcelona on only his third serious lap.

This was Rory Byrne's first Ferrari. His design philosophy is important because we have heard how John Barnard preferred rear end stability in a car while Schumacher wanted the opposite. How did Byrne approach this? 'The way John wanted the car to be set up did not, I think it's fair to say, suit Michael. I am sure Michael would have got the best out of it but he felt the car would be potentially quicker if you set it up a different way, nervous at the front. The thing is, if you think about it, front downforce comes fair-

ly drag free – you can actually set up a car so it's running more front downforce than, relatively speaking, how Barnard would want to set it up. And the overall downforce would be higher.'

This is not a criticism of him or you or anybody else, just different approaches to the same problem?

'Yes, sure, exactly. Prost wouldn't drive a car like that, he wanted to drive it the way John's described it.

'But to be honest, I design the car the way I think it's going to have the most grip, it's going to be the quickest, the best balance, the best variation in balance. The driver ends up adapting it, setting it up to suit his style, but the fundamentals – the weight distribution, the aerodynamic distribution, the sensitivity – well, I design to what I think is going to produce the quickest car.'

But you have to bear in mind that he'll be the one driving it.

'Yes.'

And the more you give him what he wants, the quicker he'll be able to go.

'Yes, sure, but what he wants is exactly what you need to go fast so there is no conflict of interests.'

And so to Melbourne for the **Australian** Grand Prix. In Friday practice, in drizzle, Schumacher was quickest but 'the weather made it difficult to do any proper set-up work. This practice was more or less a gamble. I never managed a single clear lap.' He qualified on the second row, was happy with the car although 'it is not yet at the level we intend it to be' and ran five laps of the race before the engine broke. The McLarens finished first and second.

Brazil was better, although he qualified on the second row again and said 'I think the McLarens will be unbeatable under normal circumstances but we should be the best of the rest.' He was correct. Hakkinen won from Coulthard, Schumacher third and talking of how the team had maximised what they had, but 'for Argentina we will have some developments which will allow us to challenge the McLarens. Those guys [Hakkinen and Coulthard] must be falling asleep out there.'

A miracle has happened – I'm between the McLarens and not far off pole

Initially **Argentina** seemed like Melbourne and Sao Paulo. On the Friday he was second (Coulthard 1m 28.130s, Schumacher 1m 29.114s) and 'I am happy with the new wider front tyres from Goodyear. They have helped us to close the gap. We also have some improvements on the car. Looking at the section times, I was quicker on the first section and only a couple of tenths slower in the other sections.'

He sustained that in qualifying, putting the Ferrari on the front row. 'A miracle has happened. I am between the two McLarens and not so far from pole. I feel that maybe now we can go where we want to go.'

At the red lights he had a clutch problem and was third, stalking Hakkinen, got past in a right-hander, quickly shed him and reached towards Coulthard. At 3 laps the gap was 2.139, Schumacher cutting into it. He caught Coulthard by lap 5 and into the hairpin, a slow right, Coulthard was stricken by gearbox problems, ran wide. Schumacher pressed the Ferrari's nose into the gap and Coulthard, turning in, turned into him. Coulthard spun, Schumacher continued.

'He had already run wide at that point on the previous lap so I went for the gap but he seemed to close the door. I did not want to lift off because I felt I had the momentum to get through. The car was damaged and it suffered from understeer in right-hand corners,' Schumacher said.

To compound that, he was on a two-stop strategy and the McLarens a one, obliging him to gain 20 seconds. As he took the lead he held 13 seconds over Hakkinen but the Finn was carrying plenty of speed and by lap 19 had cut it to 11.937. Schumacher set fastest lap on 23, Hakkinen bettered that on 24. Schumacher didn't find the 20 seconds and lost the lead when he pitted on lap 28. Hakkinen stayed out for another 12 laps and when he pitted Schumacher assumed the lead again. He'd make his second stop in 11 laps and needed a sprint.

	Schumacher	Hakkinen	Gain/loss
Lap 46	1: 29.386	1: 29.745	+ 0.359
Lap 47	1: 28.793	1: 29.720	– 0.073
Lap 48	1: 28.780	1: 33.174	+ 4.394

He led by 17 seconds at lap 50 and forced that to 21 seconds three laps later. As he emerged from the pit stop Hakkinen was within sight but behind back-markers. It was, or ought to have been, a milk run but on lap 67 rain fell. Schumacher went off at the final corner. He ran across gravel and rejoined.

The clarity of greatness: I lost control where the track surface was shiny but I remember Johnny Herbert going off there in the warm-up and getting stuck – so I didn't try to brake, just headed for the escape road. I'd made sure I knew where it was when we went round on the parade lap.

He beat Hakkinen by more than 20 seconds, Irvine third.

Imola and the **San Marino** Grand Prix appeared pivotal. Were Ferrari really able to match the McLarens? In Friday practice he was third. 'We are not too far from them but I don't know if they used new tyres. The situation is more difficult than I anticipated and my car is not yet set up

Contemplation, 1998. (Formula One Pictures)

properly. It was tricky to drive and unpredictable.' He qualified third behind Hakkinen. 'I lost my time on the last corner, maybe two-tenths. I aborted my second run because we had made some changes to the car and I could see they had not worked. I heard it might rain tomorrow...'

It didn't. The race is simply told, Coulthard leading throughout, Hakkinen behind him until lap 17 when the gearbox failed, Schumacher inheriting second place. 'I pushed right to the end because I do not give up until the chequered flag but I knew David was cruising.' Hakkinen 26 points, Coulthard 23, Schumacher 20, Irvine 11.

Barcelona favoured the McLarens in the **Spanish** Grand Prix. After the Friday practice he was fifth (Irvine fourth). 'Third place is the best I can hope to do in qualifying unless something unexpected happens.' He finished the race a distant third behind the McLarens.

'I made a bad start because I got too much wheelspin and I couldn't recover the situation. I lost two places but thanks to the team doing a fantastic job I moved up to third after the first pit stop. Maybe the pit lane limiter was not working properly and I saw my speed go over the limit for a moment. I came in for the [stop'n'go] penalty and was fourth behind Wurz. I pushed hard to close the gap to him and again the team called me in at just the right moment which enabled me to get past him. I don't think I could have on the track.' Hakkinen 36, Coulthard 29, Schumacher 24, Irvine 11.

Suddenly they were a third of the way through the season and the catching up was still to be done. At **Monaco** he crashed in Casino Square in practice ('I was trying too hard and lost control'), translating to fifth and moving him into the refrain: 'We are slightly behind the McLarens but the gap is not too big and this is what we expected here.' He qualified fourth and

Winter wonderland: Schumacher + snowmobile = speed, Madonna di Campiglio. (Formula One Pictures)

spoke of perhaps a place on the podium.

They ran in order Hakkinen, Coulthard, Fisichella, Schumacher. When Coulthard's engine failed on lap 18, it was Hakkinen, Fisichella, Schumacher. This held to the pit stops, Schumacher's on lap 30. He was stationary for 7.4 seconds, Fisichella pitted next lap and was stationary for 10.2. It cost Fisichella the place.

Wurz, yet to stop, held second and Schumacher drew up. At Loews Wurz seemed preoccupied with three cars pro-

ceeding nose-to-tail in front of him and seemed unaware that Schumacher was thrusting the Ferrari down the inside. The two cars rubbed wheels then, exiting the horseshoe, Wurz's front left brushed Schumacher's right rear. In a reflex action Wurz re-took Schumacher who thrust again, re-took him before the tunnel. 'I tried to pass Alex because he had left the door open. We touched, but very lightly. It was just a normal race incident and I definitely do not blame him.'

Wurz remembers this vividly, and what he is about to describe mirrors the inner conflict between following a strategy and being a racer. 'I tell you the whole story. It was the last lap before I would have come in to the pits. There were three cars in front of me, slowing each other down. Then I saw Michael coming behind me. I thought *OK, if I start to fight I will lose a lot of time* – I was racing for second position in the race at this moment. Then I saw Michael trying to overtake me. I wasn't

surprised: I was going slowly because of the three cars in front of me.

'He went on the inside and normally I would have defended my line completely to avoid any chance of him overtaking but because I was to go into the pits I didn't want to lose time, especially overall time in terms of the race. That's because you do lose more time when you fight than if you just let him go. But when he came on the inside I said to myself *oh no, I can't make it that easy for him!* So there I was on the outside and I accelerated. We touched, I think, two times because there was no space. It was not done by him on purpose and it was not done by me on purpose! Then he left me just the space of one car – the width – so I re-took him. For me this was quite a normal thing to do but I was a bit annoyed because I had lost time while this was going on. But my ego was so big I wouldn't let him past!

'Then we came to the corner before the tunnel. I wanted to be too brave and come from the outside, taking the speed into the tunnel and I forgot about Michael because I thought he'd understand I wasn't making life easy for him. I was too brave and I didn't defend my line, not even a single centimetre. And he tried it again, too aggressive for my taste because he hit me very hard. I was already in the corner and the hit was so hard it knocked the steering wheel out of my hands. I went around the corner and I felt my car was OK but I had lost a lot of time. I went into the pits and my wishbone was a little bit bent, we put in 90 kilos of fuel – I was on a one-stop strategy – and my car was too low with the bent wishbone. It was touching the ground very hard and I couldn't steer round the corners.'

Here you are, a young driver, and the great Michael Schumacher comes up behind you. What are you thinking? Are you intimidated?

'No, not at all. It's the other way round for me because with guys like Michael – or Jacques Villeneuve, for example – if you fight with them, first of all they know what they are doing, and second they are quite fair because they leave you the space: enough but not a millimetre too much!

They are not like drivers new to Formula 1 who make stupid things and you crash. Then when you fight with Michael or Jacques it makes so much fun because there is a special – well, not an agreement between us but an understanding that everyone has to live on the circuit and so we leave each other the required space: to that millimetre.' Or, as it happened, several millimetres short approaching the tunnel at Monaco …

Schumacher came into the pits prepared to retire. 'After the incident my car was damaged and I felt something wrong at the rear. I thought my race was over but the mechanics managed to change the track rod and I continued. The car was not as good as before. Having lost three laps there was not much I could do – hope for rain or some other incidents that we know can often happen here.' Hakkinen won, Schumacher tenth.

Canada started gently, Schumacher second in practice. 'Goodyear has made a good step forward. Because of this, and some improvements to the car, we appear to have partly closed the gap to the front.' He qualified third but 'I am happy, mainly because I am only two-tenths of a second behind pole. It's a long time since we have been this close.'

The race had to be re-started after Wurz crashed, and this time the bumping and boring through the initial left-right corners produced another crash. Jarno Trulli's Prost mounted the Sauber of Alesi and they came to rest like that. The race continued and Schumacher took Fisichella at the chicane to be second. The safety car came out – and Hakkinen retired, a gearbox problem. The safety car was gone by the start of lap six and Coulthard led to lap 18 when he retired, a throttle problem. Schumacher led for a lap then pitted, the safety car out again when Salo (Arrows) crashed.

Schumacher came out of the pits just as Frentzen was passing over on the far rim of the track. Schumacher moved across towards him … and across … and across, eventually forcing Frentzen into a spin and retirement. 'I do not know what happened,' Schumacher said after the race. 'If it was my fault then I want to apologise to him. I looked in the mirrors and saw nothing, then I looked to my right and still saw nothing so when I was called in for my penalty [a stop'n'go for what he'd done to Frentzen] I did not understand, as I knew I had not speeded in the pit lane.'

This penalty, on lap 35, put Schumacher third behind Fisichella and Hill. He caught Hill but as he tried to pass Hill defended his position, even giving Schumacher the elbow.

'I want to have a strong word with Hill. What he did was unacceptable. To change line once is normal but to do it three times at 320kph down the straight is very dangerous. He braked early for the first chicane and I had to cut the chicane to stop hitting him. I am very angry. You do not want to hear the words I thought in that moment because that's purely dangerous.'

When Fisichella pitted on lap 44, Schumacher sprinted.

	Schumacher	Fisichella	Gain
Lap 45	1: 19.977	1: 24.320	+ 4.343
Lap 46	1: 20.149	1: 21.921	+ 1.772
Lap 47	1: 19.610	1: 22.296	+ 2.686
Lap 48	1: 19.379	1: 22.010	+ 2.631
Lap 49	1: 20.438	1: 22.947	+ 2.509

He made up enough time to keep the lead during his second stop and won from Fisichella, Irvine third. Hakkinen 46, Schumacher 34, Coulthard 29, Irvine 19.

After the race Frank Williams protested Schumacher about what he'd done to Frentzen. Williams wasn't particularly concerned when it was rejected because 'I was making a voice heard rather than seeking redress. I felt that Michael's behaviour was out of order on the grand prix track, and it's not the first time.'

(At the drivers' briefing before the race Schumacher had asked for particular care about exiting the pit lane and, if drivers were arriving at racing speed down the track, to let them go. He also asked for a blue flag to be waved to anyone exiting the pits to warn them if a car was arriving, but in his case no blue flag was waved. He did apologise to Frentzen, explaining that he'd seen Diniz and Villeneuve and 'then there was a gap.')

Hill had pungent things to say about Schumacher.

Side-stepping these quasi-controversies, which are endemic in motor racing, Rory Byrne now takes us on a relevant detour, embracing Ayrton Senna.

Does Schumacher have an analytical ability? The difference between the great ones and the merely good is, as John Barnard has already underlined, that the great ones do it so naturally they still have brain space available.

'Yes, that's true, that's absolutely true.'

So he can come in and say X, Y or Z when he's done a really hot lap?

'Not only that but during a race. He can be turning in really quick laps *and* be on the radio asking questions or telling us various things. Most drivers don't really like to be bothered on the radio when they're really going for it, whereas he's got the mental capacity to drive quickly and still consider the other aspects of the race or whatever it is to be considered.'

I felt Michael's behaviour was out of order, and not for the first time

Even during one of the famous sprints?

'Yeah, oh yeah. He's got a bit of reserve in terms of speed and he uses it when he has to.'

And even during the sprints, when he comes on the radio or you get on the radio to him, does he still seem unhurried in his thinking?

'Sure. That's the incredible thing, and that separates the World Champions from the others. What strikes me most is not his sheer one-lap speed, because relative to people like Ayrton he's not had that many pole positions. It isn't so much his ability to put in a quick lap, which he does, it's that in qualifying quite often his very first lap is his quickest. That means he is able to find the limits straight away.'

That's not all of it …

'There are countless races where he has produced something that no-one expected. Canada, for example, when he was

Schumacher + sleigh = not so much speed. Schumacher + kart + ice = slippery skill. (Formula One Pictures)

hauled in for that 10-second penalty and everyone said "well, that's that" but he pulled back enough to win.'

Isn't it true that during a race the great ones never think they've lost, they think how do I pull it back?

'And that's how Michael thinks.'

Is he mentally strong?

'Yes he is.'

What is it that allows him to move from racing pace up to a different pace altogether...?

'... and he doesn't only do it for one lap, he can string together ten, 15 laps like that. That's what I find really amazing.'

Could Ayrton have done that?

'I don't know. When Ayrton drove for us at Toleman in 1984, the racing – relatively speaking – wasn't as competitive. You couldn't race a car on the limit for the whole race, or it was very seldom that people did. Nowadays it is much more competitive and often you do have to race pretty much on the limit the whole time. So I can't really say if Ayrton could have done it, although I think he proved when he did need to go faster that he could.'

Therefore, Byrne concludes, 'it means the great ones are racing at slightly under 100 per cent and they can step it up to 100 per cent. And as I say, Michael can keep it there for ten, 15 laps if he has to.'

In **France** everything seemed to have changed, although initially he sang the refrain after finishing fifth in practice ('as expected, after the results of last week's tests here, it seems we can now close the gap to the front'). He qualified agonisingly near pole (1m 15.159s against Hakkinen's 1m 14.929s). 'It's probably the closest gap we've ever had this year. I believe we are in a position to beat McLaren in a straight fight for the first time.'

He led the race throughout except for a single lap when he pitted, passing the lead to Irvine; paid tribute to Irvine and said *we are the best team in the pit lane.* Hakkinen 50, Schumacher 44, Coulthard 30, Irvine 25.

That was half way through the season.

The **British** Grand Prix assumed extreme importance, because if Schumacher could win there the season would tilt towards him. At one point Hakkinen had had a 17 point lead; not now. In practice Schumacher was seventh. 'I found the back of the car a bit twitchy so I am not sure if we have a problem with the car or if it's due to the change in wind conditions from those we experienced here last week [in testing].' He qualified

Precision in Australia – but this is the entrance to the pit lane! (Formula One Pictures)

second, albeit half a second slower than Hakkinen, and expressed satisfaction. 'I could have been even closer because the first section on my last run was looking good, but I locked a wheel at Abbey and ran wide. However I don't think I could have got pole.'

The race demands the most careful and sensitive dissection.

Hakkinen led from Schumacher, Coulthard third, on a track surface which was drying. On lap 5 Coulthard crowded Schumacher and overtook him. Rain fell. The order remained undisturbed to lap 38 when Coulthard spun off. By then the leaders had pitted once and now pitted again, emerging with the order still undisturbed, Hakkinen far in the lead from Schumacher. The track was deluged. Hakkinen skidded off, then wrestled the McLaren back.

At **3.15** Schumacher lapped Wurz under a stationary yellow flag: *danger, no overtaking, slow down.* To miss a flag in this

grey water murk was understandable but still required punishment. In fact Wurz didn't see the flag either – 'honestly. I didn't know a lot of the things which were happening because it was such chaos. I was happy to stay on the circuit, and I knew that Michael was behind me, so I even slowed down to give him the opportunity to overtake me. I was concentrating on my driving, I watched the mirror and saw him. I didn't race against him – if I had, I wouldn't have done what I did. So he overtook. I wasn't going really slowly but I wasn't at racing speed either. I had problems and I wanted to drive behind him because if you are behind another car and on their line there is not so much water. That was my idea. I didn't see a yellow flag at all. I was surprised [that Michael was punished]. Afterwards Jean Todt came to me and asked *did you see a yellow flag?* I replied *I'm very sorry, I didn't see any.'*

Brawn is shaking his head, waving at the stewards, saying no, no, you're wrong

At **3.16** the safety car came out and the racers bunched, following it.

The Stewards debated what to do and, from this moment onwards, Article 57 of the rules came into, and went out of, play with chaotic frequency. Section (*a*) of the Article said the Stewards must inform a team official of any infringement no later than 25 minutes 'after the moment at which the incident occurred.'

The safety car pulled off at the end of lap 49, the conditions marginally improved. Hakkinen tried to hold Schumacher at bay but the McLaren was damaged and on lap 51 Schumacher moved through, nine laps to run.

The Stewards did not record their decision – to penalise Schumacher by 10 seconds – until **3.39.**

At **3.43,** while the sodden and diminishing band of runners edged their way round lap 57 – three left to run – the Stewards' verdict was delivered to Ferrari. Crucially, it was 28 minutes after the offence.

Article 57 (*a*) also stipulates that notification of the penalty be displayed on the timing monitors, which all teams have. It wasn't.

Todt was quoted as saying that 'when the official handed us the document relating to the penalty he was unable to tell us which rule it referred to.' This provoked confusion. The difference between a 10-second stop'n'go penalty – Schumacher slowing into the pits, remaining stationary for 10 seconds, then going slowly out of the pits – would give the race to Hakkinen, but if just 10 seconds were added to Schumacher's overall race time at the end he'd win because he'd have enough of a margin in hand.

Compounding the confusion, Article 57 (*e*) stipulated that if an infringement happened 'with 12 or less complete laps remaining' the Stewards shall 'have the right to add the time penalty.' It would be no problem for Schumacher but the infringement had happened on lap 43: 17 to go.

Compounding the confusion even further, Article 57 (*b*) stipulated that if the infringement happened with more than 12 laps left 'from the time the Stewards' decision is notified on the timing monitors, the relevant driver may cover no more than three complete laps before entering the pits and proceeding to his pit where he shall remain for the period of the time penalty.' That was the 10-second stop'n'go.

Three laps remained …

Brawn was described as frantically talking to the stewards. An ITV pit lane reporter, James Allen, observed and said: 'Ross Brawn is shaking his head, waving at the stewards saying *no, no, no, you're wrong, you're wrong.'*

Todt said that 'because of the doubt' about the penalty they decided to bring Schumacher in for the stop'n'go. Beginning lap 58, as Schumacher skimmed along the start-finish straight, his crew prepared for him to come in and pay the penalty: five red-uniformed men, one holding a round sign on a pole and positioned where Schumacher would come to a halt. He completed lap 58 and moved into lap 59, his tyres stirring little rosters of spray. He had 23.414 seconds in hand.

On lap 59 he sprinted (as best he could in these conditions) because he still might need all the time he could get, the Ferrari slithering wide and coursing through standing water as he goaded it forward. The Ferrari pit, where now seven red-uniformed men stood waiting, was up towards the far end of the pit lane and you'd cross the finishing line (or rather its hypothetical extension from the track itself) to reach it.

At **3.47** the team brought him in, the Ferrari angling from the track to the long pit lane entrance. He travelled down that, along the pit lane and, just before he reached his pit, crossed the 'line.' He'd won. Hadn't he? Few could be certain of that, least of all Schumacher himself. Motionless, he served his penalty and then went out and covered another couple of laps just to be on the safe side. When all that was over, Hakkinen brought his McLaren in and sat, eyes uncomprehending. He had no idea what had hap-

pened. Nearby Schumacher embraced the Ferrari mechanics who were waving clenched fists, consumed by delight. Hakkinen 56, Schumacher 54, Coulthard 30, Irvine 29.

Before the **Austrian** Grand Prix Schumacher signed a four-year deal with Ferrari at $32 million per annum and explained that even though he'd had other proposals ('in some cases superior') he felt happy at Maranello, he and the team had done an awful lot of work and he felt optimistic about the Championship.

In Friday practice he was seventh and sang the refrain. 'We had a few more difficulties than expected. On my first run a front wheel locked up and I went off. I lost the rest of the session while the mechanics worked on the car to repair the damage from the gravel trap. In the afternoon I had a similar situation, this time a rear wheel locked up.'

He qualified fourth in a session which began under heavy rain and ended dry-

A unique photograph. Schumacher wins the British Grand Prix in the pits. (Formula One Pictures)

ing, Fisichella pole from Alesi, then Hakkinen and Schumacher. 'We had planned to stay on wets but when we saw other drivers improving their times on intermediates we decided to fit the same. This took some time because we changed the settings, so I went out late and couldn't get the best time out of the car.'

A turbulent first lap settled to Hakkinen leading from Schumacher, the safety car out. Schumacher was on a two-stop strategy, Hakkinen only one, lending an imperative for Schumacher to overtake and build a lead when the safety car pulled off. He attacked, Hakkinen resisted and in a right-hander Schumacher locked brakes, ran wide, resumed third behind Fisichella. He stole inside Fisichella and caught Hakkinen again, setting fastest lap. They duelled until lap 17 when, at the last corner – a descending arc of a right – Schumacher ran wide at the exit, bounding across grass and gravel, battering bits off the Ferrari. 'I lost control because I was going too quickly. It was a stupid mistake. As the car jumped through the gravel and I lost the front wing I thought there was more damage but the car proved to be very strong.' He completed a full, and laborious, lap to reach the pits and changing the nosecone took 19.3 seconds. He was last.

He put together a sustained recovery so that by lap 34 he was in the points, and by lap 68 (of 71) on the podium – overtaking Irvine, who slowed with a reported brake problem. Team orders? But they'd been banned since Melbourne when Coulthard allowed Hakkinen to win under a gentleman's agreement, hadn't they? Irvine was diplomatic and spoke of Inspector Clouseau solving this particular mystery. Hakkinen 66, Schumacher 58, Coulthard 36, Irvine 32.

Layers of pressure hemmed him at Hockenheim where, in practice for the **German** Grand Prix, he was fifth and spoke of how bumpy the track surface was. He qualified ninth and 'of course I am disappointed.' In the race he finished fifth, 'the best I could do. My main problem was lack of grip in the Motodrom [the stadium section] where it was difficult to simply keep the car on the road.' Hakkinen 76, Schumacher 60, Coulthard 42, Irvine 32.

The Hungaroring is, or was, exactly where you can't do much except go round and round. Apart from the long straight it's corner after corner where you're obliged to play follow-my-leader. The scope for creativity is, or was, so limited that before 16 August 1998 people didn't think in those terms at all. They saw it as a place held rigid by orthodoxy: qualify well then settle fatalistically to the going round and round with, maybe, an overtaking move or two at the end of the straight.

Across the 77 laps of the **Hungarian** Grand Prix, Brawn and Schumacher would banish historical precedent, bend the rigidity to their will and ultimately redefine the possible.

In Friday practice Schumacher was third. 'We are in much better shape than in Hockenheim. The gap to the front runners is not too big.' He qualified third behind the McLarens. 'With the right strategy we have a chance in the race and I believe we will make the most of it.'

Ferrari and McLaren would adopt the same strategies, however, both intending to pit twice. Hakkinen led the race from Coulthard, Schumacher third and needing to deal with Coulthard to get after Hakkinen. Precedent held so far, the race static. At lap 14 Coulthard was at 2.426 seconds from Hakkinen and Schumacher at 3.649. Schumacher pitted first but emerged behind Villeneuve, Coulthard pitting next lap, Hakkinen two laps later. Hakkinen kept the lead, Coulthard kept second place, Schumacher still behind Villeneuve and to underscore Schumacher's captivity Coulthard set fastest lap. The McLarens were romping it.

Brawn now made a profound decision: we'll move to three stops. When this was radioed to Schumacher he thought 'I'm not sure if it will work.'

Brawn conceded that the new strategy was aggressive but 'we had nothing to lose.'

Villeneuve pitted on lap 31, releasing Schumacher who set fastest lap and cut into the gaps. Coulthard was 2.2 seconds ahead and Hakkinen 6.1. This was going to be arm-wrestling.

	Schumacher	Hakkinen	Coulthard
Lap 32	1: 19.952	1: 21.187	1: 21.184
Lap 33	1: 20.187	1: 21.512	1: 20.852
Lap 34	1: 20.360	1: 20.845	1: 20.704
Lap 35	1: 20.480	1: 21.213	1: 21.175
Lap 36	1: 21.190	1: 21.456	1: 21.153

By half distance Schumacher had pressed Coulthard up towards Hakkinen and three seconds covered them all. Schumacher harried Coulthard to lap 43, when he – Schumacher – pitted and was stationary for 6.8 seconds. Coulthard pitted next lap and, straining towards the tip of the pit lane, watched Schumacher go by. Schumacher's lap before his stop had been a 1:21. Now he pounded the Hungaroring, on lap 45 going below 1:20 for the first time – 1:19.918, then 1:19.594. That was lap 46 – Hakkinen pitting. Hakkinen led by 23 seconds: enough to retain the lead? He came in on lap 46, and as Schumacher went by he was only half way down the pit lane. Schumacher led the race because he'd been stationary a shorter time – and he'd been that because the team didn't need to put enough fuel in to get him to the end, not with another stop to come.

Neither of the McLarens was far behind.

The Ferrari radio crackled and Brawn said the fateful words which, in time, will pass into grand prix mythology if they haven't already. 'You have 19 laps to build a 25-second lead.'

Schumacher replied: 'Thank you very much.'

He forced it as hard and far as it was possible to do: his phrase. He was about to put together one of the most sustained periods of speed which grand prix racing has ever seen.

	Schumacher	Hakkinen
Lap 47	1: 20.694	1: 42.419

That was after Hakkinen's pit stop, the real struggle for the soul of the race about to begin. The overall column is how much Schumacher increased his lead from lap 48 to Brawn's demand of 25 seconds. Fasten your seat belts …

	Schumacher	Hakkinen	Gain/Loss	Overall
Lap 48	1: 19.805	1: 22.285	+ 2.480	+ 2.480
Lap 49	1: 20.640	1: 22.276	+ 1.636	+ 4.116
Lap 50	1: 21.286	1: 22.215	+ 0.929	+ 5.045
Lap 51	1: 20.302	1: 22.851	+ 2.549	+ 7.594
Lap 52	1: 25.822	1: 25.593	− 0.229	+ 7.365

On that lap the depth of the forcing took him off the track at the right-handed curve onto the start-finish straight, across grass, smearing the tyres with dry mud as, ferocious, he came back on. He'd been forcing too hard: his phrase again. He did not know that Hakkinen was finding the McLaren almost impossible to drive with some undiagnosed problem, or that Coulthard – now past Hakkinen on lap 52 – had a problem with a rear tyre. In fact, the new strategy was so subtle and working itself out so fast that Schumacher didn't even know he was in the lead when he went off. Crossing the line to complete this lap Schumacher led Coulthard by 10.897.

He drove on the limit, his race became three sprints, and that's hard

	Schumacher	Coulthard	Gain/Loss	Overall
Lap 53	1: 20.672	1: 23.670	+ 2.998	+ 13.895
Lap 54	1: 19.857	1: 21.677	+ 1.820	+ 15.715
Lap 55	1: 21.005	1: 21.250	+ 0.245	+ 15.960
Lap 56	1: 20.163	1: 21.475	+ 1.312	+ 17.272

He was flicking the Ferrari through the twitchy sequence of corners towards the curve to the start-finish straight, commanding it across the kerbs, skimming a little smoke from the tyres as the brakes dug. He was spreading mastery across the whole circuit.

	Schumacher	Coulthard	Gain/Loss	Overall
Lap 57	1: 20.106	1: 21.377	+ 1.271	+ 18.543
Lap 58	1: 19.625	1: 22.162	+ 2.537	+ 21.080
Lap 59	1: 19.966	1: 21.658	+ 1.692	+ 22.772

On lap 60 Schumacher forced the Ferrari towards what must have been the ultimate

A fraught practice at Hockenheim when the engine lets go. (Formula One Pictures)

OVERLEAF: *With Irvine at Monza. Communion?* (Formula One Pictures)

even he could draw from it. He set a new fastest lap and now you could see the consequences of the forcing. The car shivered and danced and vibrated, his helmet was bobbing, his hands were pumping. He was carving through the corners.

Even Brawn watched stunned: his word.

	Schumacher	Coulthard	Gain/Loss	Overall
Lap 60	1: 19.286	1: 21.213	+ 1.927	+ 24.699
Lap 61	1: 19.510	1: 21.427	+ 1.917	+ 26.616

The Ferrari mechanics trundled fresh tyres into position and began to man the refuelling rig. Schumacher dipped the car into the pit lane, was stationary for 7.7 seconds and as he accelerated onto the track Coulthard was on the horizon – *back* on the horizon.

Fifteen laps remained and across them Schumacher made no mistake, beating Coulthard by nearly ten seconds. It was a rout, an intellectual rout, although Schumacher rationed euphoria. It was, he'd say, 'one of my most emotional' victories. Hakkinen 77, Schumacher 70, Coulthard 48, Irvine 32.

Nigel Stepney gives the race its proper context. 'You need to look more and more each year for advantages, and that's the problem, because there are a lot less now than there used to be. Hungary was down to strategy but that meant a *lot* of pressure on the driver. He was made to drive on the limit and his race became three sprints. That's the hardest thing. There's a lot of pressure in the strategies to push the driver as much as you can, and you are going to make mistakes because it's sprinting, it's not behaving as you do in normal racing conditions.'

If Brawn makes a specific demand Schumacher meets it.

'Yes, because Michael believes in that strategy and he goes with it.'

Stepney, like Barnard and Byrne, emphasises the absolute importance of the mental aspect and the advantage that brings.

'The top drivers spend very little time thinking about what they are doing. Their driving a racing car is as natural to them as you getting in your car and going to the shops. Other racing drivers are thinking about other things too much, they're thinking about everything – the person in front, the braking and so on. With Michael that's in a second memory, if you like. The rest of it is concentrated on pushing to get the best out of the car, and feeling the car, and getting the maximum performance out of himself as well.

'If you see Hakkinen when he gets out of a car after a race, he's been sweating a lot. Michael – not a bead. I've seen him sweat once, I think. He's *so* cool when he gets out of the car. You saw Hakkinen at Monza [in 1999], he was completely soaked with sweat. Michael I have never seen like that. Never.'

Yes, but if Brawn gets on the radio and says you have 19 laps to gain 25 seconds, where do those seconds come from?

'You have to have the car ... well, you have to have everything, the strategy, somebody with the potential to do that strategy, and the capability yourself.'

He doesn't just find it for one lap ...

'No, no, he finds it all the time. Some drivers overdrive a lot and I'll give you an instance of what that can mean. We asked Michael to back off in one race and he went quicker, so we radioed and said *we asked you to back off*. He replied *but I have backed off!* The reason he was actually going faster was that in backing off he suddenly had more momentum going on the car rather than pushing it and pulling it. This can work the other way. Sometimes the more you ask them to push the slower they go, whereas that time Michael relaxed it a little bit and he was smoother, using less fuel, less brakes and going quicker.

'For some drivers, this sort of thing can be a problem in qualifying. You see some of them pushing like hell and they're pushing too much. If they just drove as they had in the morning session, when they weren't under pressure, 50 per cent of them would achieve better lap times. The only people who can do banzai laps are the Sennas and Schumachers [*banzai* = one qualifying lap of total speed regardless of consequences]. Well, Berger did a few and Mansell could produce them. Prost was quick but he couldn't do that. Senna always wanted to be quickest, *booof.* That's not true of Michael. For Senna it was a physical and psychological thing to be quickest, a need to give himself that push, and also psychological against his competitors.'

And another interesting detour ...

Senna took a record 65 pole positions from his 161 grands prix but set only 19 fastest laps. By the end of 1999 Schumacher had taken 23 pole positions from 128 grands prix with 39 fastest laps. Senna set so many poles and won the races from there, and maybe set so few fastest laps because, courtesy of the poles, he placed himself in positions where he didn't need to. Schumacher has set comparatively few poles but proved again and again that advantages can still be found. Like the Hungaroring, 16 August 1998 ...

Belgium was the epi-centre of several storms, and the weather wasn't very good either. In Friday practice he was first, qualified fourth next day and wasn't happy to be 'over one second off pole'. Race day was wet and on the first lap a vast, churning accident developed on the descent towards Eau Rouge. At the re-start Hill led but round La Source Schumacher and Hakkinen bumped, the McLaren spinning. Helplessly Herbert rammed it.

'I was on the outside and I tried to leave a bit of room,' Schumacher would say. 'He was forcing me a bit wide but I had the better line and could accelerate better out of the corner.'

He advanced on Hill but the safety car came out, circled and released them into lap 3. He advanced on Hill again and on lap 8 stole nimbly inside at the Bus Stop. Far, far behind – second last, in fact – Coulthard ploughed through the water. He'd skimmed off just before the safety car arrived. Schumacher pitted and resumed in the lead, Hill too far away to pose any threat. The rain now shrouded Spa. Cars loomed and lurked within the shroud, emerging and returning. Somewhere in this was Coulthard, last

because he'd just made a pit stop. Schumacher was headed towards disaster.

	Schumacher	Coulthard	Gain
Lap 20	2: 11.135	2: 16.679	+ 5.544
Lap 21	2: 11.010	2: 18.284	+ 7.274
Lap 22	2: 13.671	2: 16.824	+ 3.153
Lap 23	2: 16.420	2: 16.601	+ 0.181

Schumacher completed lap 24 in 2:14.504 and moved into his 25th lap. Coulthard, so far behind, moved into his 24th lap. Schumacher was almost 2 minutes 14 seconds ahead of Coulthard and therefore seeking to lap him. Todt made his way down the pit lane to McLaren to point this out. Schumacher reached Coulthard, tried to harry him and – according to one report – waved his arm, meaning *get out of the way.*

Subsequently Ferrari put this into words. 'For almost an entire lap, Coulthard ignored the blue flags [another competitor is trying to overtake you] and never allowed Schumacher to go by ... on several occasions Schumacher moved off line to show Coulthard he was there.'

> A phalanx of Ferrari people formed a wall between him and Coulthard

Schumacher's urgency was surprising because he led Hill by 34 seconds, ample time to make his second pit stop (scheduled for the next lap). Ron Dennis radioed to Coulthard, saying *let him go,* to which Coulthard replied that in the shroud he could see virtually nothing and asked exactly where Schumacher was. Coulthard then eased off and positioned the McLaren over to the right on the approach to the left-hander Pouhon corner. Unfortunately that was the racing line ...

Schumacher ran full into the back of him, the impact a shocking moment, severe enough to pluck the Ferrari's right-front wheel clean off. Schumacher continued to the pits on three wheels, wild with rage. He sprang from the cockpit and marched down the pit lane, tearing his helmet off as he went, to confront Coulthard. A Ferrari employee tried to restrain him but couldn't.

By the time he'd reached the McLaren pit a phalanx of five or six Ferrari people, Todt among them, formed a wall between him and Coulthard.

'Are you [expletive] trying to kill me?' he shouted across to Coulthard.

The phalanx ushered him off and he walked stiffly back up the pit lane, his face now consumed by the rage.

Later he said Coulthard 'seemed to be running 5 to 6 seconds slower than his real pace once I was behind him. Obviously lifting on the straight like he did when I hit him is very dangerous. He has the experience to know that you do not slow down on a straight like that without giving any warning. So one could think he did it deliberately.'

The unstated implication, of course, was that Coulthard had in some devilish way done this to help Hakkinen's chase for the Championship. That made Coulthard angry enough to say any such accusation was 'paranoia in the extreme' and Schumacher needed 'to get some help for controlling his anger.'

When Schumacher calmed down he accepted that he had 'over-reacted' but still insisted Coulthard made a mistake 'because it was clear he was going slower than normal and it was the wrong place at the wrong time to let someone through. No-one could expect it there.'

Since Irvine had spun off after 25 laps the leader board was undisturbed – Hakkinen 77, Schumacher 70, Coulthard 48, Irvine 32. Next came Monza, the **Italian** Grand Prix and the assumed annual communion next.

The Friday was wet, Irvine was quickest and Schumacher second. 'I wasn't able to do many laps. I had a leaking brake pipe and there was a problem with the steering system. All the same, we looked quite competitive.' On the Saturday he took pole, his first of the season. 'We got everything right and picked the best moment to go out. I did my time on the first lap of my final run. I hadn't expected it to be good enough because my last lap should have been the quickest but on that lap I made a mistake …'

The pole secured, the session completed, he stood on the pit lane wall facing the grandstands opposite and raised his arms, blew a kiss, waved with his left hand. Communion?

He made a poor start to the race ('everything that could go wrong did go wrong') and ran fifth, Hakkinen leading from Coulthard, Irvine third, Villeneuve fourth. Like in Hungary, Schumacher seemed lost in captivity, the McLarens romping it already – except that Monza is neither rigid nor static.

He moved inside Villeneuve at the second chicane but, completing this opening lap, the McLarens were clear. Romping it. Irvine let him through but at lap 5 the gap was out to 4.567. He accelerated, set fastest lap and next time round had sliced the gap to 3.670. Without warning Hakkinen waved Coulthard through – Hakkinen wasn't happy with the car. Quickly Schumacher caught Hakkinen, but if and when he dealt with him Coulthard, who'd already opened the gap to 9.3, would be another matter.

Monza is not precisely as you see it on television. There are banks of tall trees which give it a pastoral depth and a parkland charm but there is also an air of mystery because so many grandstands are partially obscured by the trees, so many of the teeming *tifosi* thousands are unseen. They are *so* many and *so* teeming that the noises they make rise in choral thunder and are taken up by the thousands over here through these trees, and the thousands over there through those.

Monza is a dangerous forest.

On lap 17 Coulthard's engine failed and he swivelled the car off. The thunder from the thousands reverberated into the trees and reverberated back.

Schumacher pressured Hakkinen at the second chicane and overtook him on the exit. Hakkinen proffered a reflex counter-attack but Schumacher had the lead. The thunder reverberated into the

The podium at Monza, trying to disprove Newton's Theory of gravity – and nearly doing it. (Formula One Pictures)

trees again and came back like an immense wall of sound.

Monza surrendered and the emotions were heightened when Irvine came home second. To complete the day Hakkinen had brake problems, spun late on and finished fourth. You could sense from the thousands gathering below the podium – *so teeming that the track submerged beneath them for a hundred metres in either direction – a strong, living feeling. The Championship, denied them since that day when Jo-dee passed where they now stood, was on.*

We will certainly not give up – we can still win in Japan

Hakkinen and Schumacher 80; with Coulthard (48) and Irvine (38) no longer contenders.

The **Luxembourg** Grand Prix was at the Nürburgring, theoretically favouring Schumacher. He was fourth on the Friday but 'I am not concerned about the time differences because I only used one set of tyres.' He took pole, Irvine alongside, Hakkinen third.

Irvine led from Schumacher, Hakkinen third and that was exactly what Hakkinen did not want. Irvine would let Schumacher through then block and balk while Schumacher sailed off into the sunset. Schumacher went past Irvine on the opening lap but Hakkinen was phlegmatic, hustled Irvine and on lap 14 slipstreamed him into the chicane. Hakkinen remained phlegmatic and gradually increased his pace so that when Schumacher pitted on lap 24 the gap had fallen to five seconds. As Schumacher pitted Hakkinen behaved as the thinking drivers do.

Sprint …

Hakkinen sustained that for the next three laps, set a new fastest lap and led by 17.037. He emerged from his stop directly in front of Schumacher, the decisive moment of the race and of enormous significance for the Championship because only Suzuka remained. Hakkinen 90, Schumacher 86.

'I am a little bit disappointed because I thought we could win here,' Schumacher said. 'Unfortunately we weren't quick enough. I couldn't push as hard as I wanted because the technical package was not perfect. Four points is not an impossible difference. We will certainly not give up because we can still win in Japan.'

People who enjoy these things worked on the many permutations, but mercifully – like Jerez in 1997 – they devolved into simplicity. If Hakkinen won the **Japanese** Grand Prix or came second he was World Champion. If he finished third, fourth or fifth, Schumacher had to win.

On the Friday, Schumacher was quickest (Hakkinen fifth) and restricted himself to Press Release-speak. 'We got through all the work on our programme for today and made some good progress with the set-up. Of course I am happy to be on provisional pole but I do not think today's result shows the whole truth and therefore I expect qualifying to be very close. I believe we are competitive. All the hard work in testing over the past few weeks seems to have paid off.'

In qualifying they danced a desperate duet.

Hakkinen, out early, did a 1m 37.095s – a full second and a half quicker than anybody else.

Schumacher wasn't surprised and said he'd foreseen something like it. Mid-way through the session he gave his response, an almost sensuous lap of power and poise: 1m 36.769s.

Hakkinen tried to respond but couldn't find the final fractions: 1m 36.855s.

Now Schumacher summoned a 1m 36.293.

Hakkinen tried to respond to that but, moving under the weight gathering over him if he failed – pole might be crucial – went off onto grass, the lap destroyed.

Schumacher had pole, Hakkinen alongside, Coulthard and Irvine on the

Schumacher stalls at the start at Suzuka – look for the man with the yellow flag – and the restart, Schumacher (centre of the track) already gaining places. (Formula One Pictures)

The puncture finally decided the Championship.
(Formula One Pictures)

second row. 'Of course it is nice to be in pole position but this is only qualifying and we must not get too excited about it.'

On the grid Hakkinen went over and shook Schumacher's hand, reflecting the tone of the season. Whatever Schumacher's ambition and abilities had brought in the battles against Senna, Hill, Villeneuve and Coulthard, his experiences with Hakkinen had been precisely the same as everybody else's. No problem.

A dry afternoon at Suzuka, warm, sunny. They moved into the parade lap, that curious state of suspended animation, that weaving crocodile which expands and contracts on its journey back round to the grid. They settled but no red lights came, only three flashing yellows: *start aborted*. Trulli, on the seventh row, had stalled his Prost.

The mechanics poured onto the grid to do their work.

The second parade lap was six or seven minutes later. Because a grand prix car is at once extremely robust and extremely delicate, and much happier at 200mph than motionless, this was a period of danger. The cars had been on the grid, covered a lap, returned and were about to cover another lap, all in high temperatures. Schumacher led them away again and went round at a pace rather more than sprightly, then slowed. The crocodile broke up as the cars peeled off to their bays. The last of the 21 – Trulli, now at the rear – took his place. Then, from the pit lane wall, a yellow flag was being waved: *start aborted*.

Schumacher's right hand was up, the international signal for *I can't move*. He shook his head in disbelief. 'The engine stalled because the clutch didn't free itself and I don't know why.' What he did know was that the whole thing would have to be gone through again and he'd be at the back behind Trulli. The Championship had saved this last, savage twist until now, or so we thought.

Hakkinen took them round a third time, Schumacher a lonely vision at the rear. They settled again, waited again, and the red lights blinked on, blinked off. Finally they accelerated away. Hakkinen led from Irvine while in that other, lowly world at the back of the grid Schumacher fed the power into the Ferrari and took it to mid track, pointing it directly ahead like a missile. And it travelled like a missile, gathering speed. Along the straight towards the first corner it bisected Trulli and Esteban Tuero's Minardi; bisected Shinji Nakano's Minardi and Herbert's Sauber ('I'd stalled as well'). It powered clean round Toranosuke Takagi's Tyrrell.

I was curious about how a driver thinks when he's sitting on the grid knowing that the moment they all set off Schumacher will be coming like a tornado. Does the driver worry about that? 'No,' says Herbert. 'No, no, no. You're trying to do what you are going to do yourself, never mind about him.' But you know he'll be coming? 'No you don't. He might stall again. And if he does, and you're thinking he'll be coming through … you might stall.' But you did stall! [LAUGHTER] And the start Schumacher made? 'It was a ridiculous start, I've never seen a start like that in my life. He just took off.'

Crossing the line to complete the opening lap, Schumacher was twelfth, 9.663 seconds from Hakkinen.

On lap 2, he despatched Panis and Alesi, and that was tenth.

On lap 3, on the long right curve after the hairpin, he out-powered Fisichella, and that was ninth, 11.784 seconds from Hakkinen.

On lap 4 he pressured Wurz, then took a sling-shot wide through the S curves, and that was eighth.

On lap 5 he caught and despatched his brother (who, incidentally, did not simply scamper out of the way but made him work), and that was seventh, the gap 12.580 seconds.

He was in among the faster men and couldn't pick them off one a lap, something compounded by the fact that the full-attack he'd mounted would have to be paid for in tyre wear and he was beginning to pay. He spent long minutes behind Hill and Villeneuve, and at 8 laps the gap was out to 18.680. It kept rising towards half a minute.

On lap 14 Hill pitted, and that was sixth.

He despatched Villeneuve round the outside at the hairpin, and that was fifth.

On lap 16 he'd caught Coulthard but came in for his first pit stop. It cost him only one place, to Villeneuve, and that was sixth.

Across the next four laps others pitted, too: Villeneuve, Frentzen, Coulthard. Each moved Schumacher up a place so that by lap 22 he was third, 26 seconds from Hakkinen. He ran third to lap 31.

The last, savage twist had not been the stalling on the grid. It was now. He was taking the Ferrari into the corner after the pits, his speed reaching towards 170mph when the right rear tyre disintegrated. He did not lose control of the car but managed to slow it, parking on the grass. A great calmness descended on him. He clambered out of the cockpit and levered himself up on to a wall, spectated just like everybody else; lowered himself from the wall, stood, spectated again. The toil of a whole season had been reduced to this: proximity to the great prize, then it was gone, completely gone.

Why did Schumacher stall? Rory Byrne explains that 'it wasn't a fault by Michael, it was something that happened with the hydraulic system.'

Why had the tyre punctured? Takagi and Tuero crashed, spreading debris everywhere, and Schumacher had run over it.

'We were *that* close to the Championship and we *could* actually have won it, yes, yes,' Byrne says.

There is no particular regret in his voice as he speaks these words, because he's an old hand who knows the score. You can't ever master everything, can't ever give absolute guarantees about every part on the stressed machine, can't make tyres which will never puncture.

There is perhaps a nuance of regret mingled with a certain pride as Byrne reflects on 1998. 'It was a hell of a season! We and Goodyear definitely started off behind McLaren by a reasonable margin [McLaren on Bridgestones] but by the end of the year we were at least as quick, if not quicker. Take the last three races: we were on pole for each – and even if you take Hakkinen's qualifying and add Coulthard's, then take Michael and Eddie's qualifying, you'll find that as a team we out-qualified McLaren over those races. We were running really quick, we'd come from way behind to be at least as quick. It was pleasing.

'We did a massive amount of development. I think the people here at Maranello were surprised at how much we did and how many new things we put on the car through the season. The reason we did that is we started the car relatively late, not because we wanted to but because we were still assembling the people. We really didn't have the depth of research to put into the car then. We were developing it rapidly through the season, and that's exactly what paid off at the end.'

But the Horse remained untamed.

chapter five

The $2 billion role reversal? (1999)

The new Ferrari, the F399, was launched in late January. Maranello was even more determined on success than in 1998. Todt stated that the objective was no longer a few pole positions and a few wins scattered across another season of prelude: the objective was the title. There was an imperative: *we have to be on the pace immediately, we can't afford another start like last year when the McLarens ran away from us.* Schumacher emphasised that in his own precise language. 'I cannot win the title if I am not able to be competitive in the first five grands prix.'

He tested the car at Fiorano, covering 57 laps and making Press Release noises, but when they went to Barcelona Hakkinen was half a second quicker in the new McLaren.

'What happened,' Byrne says, 'is that we got caught up in a massive race for the Championship in 1998 so we actually started the 1999 car too late. It's the perennial problem in that you have to concentrate both on the car you have and the car for next season, and you only have X number of resources, X number of hours in the day. It's a fine balance.'

The **Australian** Grand Prix at Melbourne was strictest reality. In the Friday untimed session Schumacher was seventh, two and a half seconds away from Hakkinen, fastest, and would speak of a problem with first gear, of the eternal and elusive search to set the car up properly. In qualifying he improved to third, narrowing the gap to less than a second and a half.

'We have encountered some problems with our car here which we hadn't in winter testing. This prevented us from making use of the full performance potential which is definitely there. We know which areas we have to work on before the next race to unlock that potential. We have concentrated on the car's reliability and that is a crucial factor for the race so there is no need to be pessimistic.'

Moving from the grid into the parade lap he couldn't engage first gear and had to begin from the back. He rose robustly to fourth despite gear selection problems, went off and had a puncture, pitted and resumed last, pitted again to change the steering wheel because 'occasionally it caused the gearbox to slip into neutral.' He finished eighth (something lost under the weight of the celebrations for Irvine, rejoicing at his first win) and expressed unhappiness with his race although he drew a measure of comfort from the fact that both Ferraris did finish, making it 'a better start than last year. To be honest, at that first race we really didn't know how to get the best out of the car and although we won it we weren't on McLaren's pace.'

After the untimed session in **Brazil** 'we look in better shape than we did in Melbourne.' He was fifth, slightly over a second slower than Coulthard, fastest, and that endured into qualifying. 'I did not expect to be one second off the pole time. We had hoped to be competitive right from the start of the season and it seems we have not achieved that. It is unlikely we can close the gap between now and the race.'

He was right, although he finished second to Hakkinen and that left him 'very satisfied. It was not what we expected after qualifying. I am not worried about the points situation because we are still at a very early stage in the season.'

His words are almost robotic in their predictability. He was trawling the same territory time after time, year after year. How else could he capture the repetitive character of the situations in which he found himself?

For **San Marino** he'd been saying there'd be 'new developments' for the car which, finally, would enable it to run with the McLarens.

In the untimed session Schumacher was third but now less than half a second from Coulthard and very, very close to Hakkinen; in qualifying closer still. 'This is a lot better than Brazil, because being only two tenths behind pole (Hakkinen 1m 26.362, Coulthard 1m 26.384s, Schumacher 1m 26.538s) is closer than I had expected, but I am a bit disappointed with my own performance. I did not manage a perfect lap. I could have gone better and pole position was within reach.'

Todt would say: 'The only way to win was to go for a slightly risky strategy …'

Hakkinen led from Coulthard and Schumacher who briefly harried Coulthard but he drew away and, within a few laps, Hakkinen was clear of them both. Schumacher concentrated on 'keeping the gap to Coulthard under control.'

The sheer scale of the team effort. Ferrari, 1999. (Formula One Pictures)

That was the best he could hope for, maybe somehow getting second place.

At the end of lap 17, in the right-hander onto the start-finish straight, Hakkinen made a mistake, the car rode over the kerbing, spun and speared the barrier so Coulthard led, Schumacher cutting the gap from 4.4 seconds to 3.9 to 3.7. As Coulthard and Schumacher hammered towards half distance Brawn began to explore the flexibility.

The clarity of greatness: if we make one stop we will finish second. If we make two stops – with a sprint in between – we could outrun Coulthard even though he's only stopping once, get out ahead; and even if it goes wrong we'll still be second.

Schumacher's on-board radio crackled. He accelerated, moving into qualifying mode. You could feel the intensity of the hunt, feel him wrenching the Ferrari through the corners.

	Coulthard	Schumacher	Gain
Lap 28	1m 29.706s	1m 29.435s	+ 0.271
Lap 29	1m 29.840s	1m 29.269s	+ 0.571
Lap 30	1m 30.953s	1m 29.599s	+ 1.354

He pitted on lap 31, was stationary for 6.9 seconds, received fresh tyres.

When Coulthard pitted his lead had been reduced to 18.3 seconds. As he nosed from the pit lane Schumacher was in traffic but going by. Coulthard got trapped behind Panis and Fisichella. Schumacher pulled away, as he had to do.

	Schumacher	Coulthard	Gain
Lap 36	1m 30.063s	1m 54.249s (pits)	
Lap 37	1m 29.095s	1m 30.694s	+ 1.599
Lap 38	1m 29.382s	1m 31.739s	+ 2.357

Coulthard took Panis but locked brakes. Panis moved ahead again, disturbing the whole race by doing what he was entitled to do: minding his own business. As Ken Tyrrell used to say, *it's up to them to get past you, not the other way round.*

By lap 41 Schumacher had extended the lead to 16.014 and still Coulthard was behind Panis who did move over, allowing Coulthard to reach Fisichella. Schumacher set fastest lap, 1:28.609.

Coulthard squeezed past Fisichella. Schumacher pitted on lap 45 with a lead of 21.8, was stationary for 5.5 seconds and came out ahead. Schumacher, fielding the *tifosi*'s rapture at this unexpected home win, would pay his tributes, explaining that one of Ferrari's strengths was its 'tactical possibilities.' Ferrari's last Imola victory was 16 years before, when Patrick Tambay won from Alain Prost. Schumacher now inherited the championship lead from Irvine.

Gazing ahead from Imola, Byrne feels 'there is no doubt that by the time the European part of the season started we'd got on the pace. If you look at Imola, Monaco, Barcelona and Magny-Cours we were not just on the pace but within a couple of tenths of a second from McLaren. It was very close, that's for sure.'

At **Monaco** in the Thursday session Schumacher was quickest and described the driving as 'good fun' although 'I hit the barrier after a track rod broke in the chicane. This was a bit frightening.' Schumacher, who had won here three times before, qualified second (Hakkinen pole), setting the time on his first run. 'I was blocked by another car on my third run and on my fourth I had to slow down at Tabac corner because of yellow flags so I could not improve.'

At the lights he surged round the outside of Hakkinen into Ste. Devote and, completing this opening lap, led by 1.398. He was muscling Monaco and would lead every lap of the race. This was not the sprint of Imola, this was remorseless, overwhelming. By the pit stop on lap 42 he had a lead of more than 20 seconds and Hakkinen lost time in a spin. 'After the stop I was able to take it easy and just bring the car home.' Schumacher was now the most successful Ferrari grand prix driver of all time, with 16 wins. Irvine finished second, Hakkinen third, and that

An Italian television lady gets her interview. (Andreas Beil/ATP)

> ## This was not the sprint of Imola, this was remorseless, overwhelming

gave the Championship an inviting look: Schumacher 26 points, Irvine 18, Hakkinen 14.

What should have been the central core of the season proved straightforward. **Spain,** when he finished third, was a bore of a race and everyone agreed that. Some alert observer noted that of the 22 starters only two managed overtaking moves in the whole 65 laps. The culprit, the drivers all agreed, was the hard, grooved tyres which reduced grip and the possibilities of overtaking. Hakkinen won.

> **When he hit the tyres the whole crowd just went deathly quiet**

In **Canada** Schumacher took his first pole of 1999 and led to lap 29. 'I lost control of the car at the last chicane because I went off the racing line, got on the dirt and ended up in the wall. This was clearly my mistake. I apologise to the team.' He added 'I usually make one mistake a year' and hoped this had been it. Hakkinen won, giving him the Championship lead with 34 points, Schumacher 30, Irvine 25.

In **France** he qualified sixth in heavy rain after 'a chaotic session. Track conditions were very dangerous with a lot of aquaplaning and there was a risk of spinning even on the straights.' He described the race as 'chaotic' too. 'My radio stopped working early on so I tried to communicate with the pits with hand signals. My first problem was that I was having trouble changing gear and the reason I slowed a lot at one point was that I only had first and second. So I came in and changed the steering wheel but from this point on things did not really improve. The new set of tyres did not work. I am not sure why. At the end of the race I had a fight with my brother Ralf like in our old karting days …'

He was fifth. Frentzen won, restricting Hakkinen to six points and that kept Schumacher in touch. Hakkinen 40, Schumacher 32, Irvine 26.

In **Britain** he was sixth on the Friday, and spoke of improvements being carried

out. 'Because of this, I am confident we can have a good weekend.'

He qualified second to Hakkinen. 'My last lap could have been quicker and reduced the gap but I lost the back end of the car [putting two wheels off]. Even so I don't think it would have been good enough to take pole but we are looking in good shape for the race.' Irvine was on the second row, alongside Coulthard.

It was hot and sunny, a halcyon midsummer race day. The five red lights blinked off after three seconds, Hakkinen away fast, Coulthard behind, then Irvine, then Schumacher, but two cars stalled on the grid. Through Becketts, Schumacher hustled Irvine and they moved onto Hangar Straight abreast. As they reached Stowe corner Irvine positioned his Ferrari over towards the left preparing to go round the right-hander, Schumacher inside him. At this moment the Stewards decided to stop the race because of the two stalled cars but, crucially, the drivers couldn't know that yet.

At racing speed Schumacher moved to mid track, Irving comfortably on the outside. Schumacher was doing 191mph (307kph) and it seemed Irvine was obeying the constrictions of his Ferrari contract by letting Schumacher through. Certainly, turning into Stowe, Schumacher was ahead – but he was locking wheels.

The brakes clawed the speed down. The FIA would describe what happened next graphically enough, once the Ferrari's black box had been downloaded. 'He first braked at 306kph and achieved an initial deceleration of 3.1G. This fell to 2.1G. At 204kph the front wheels locked.'

He shrieked across in front of Irvine and smoke billowed from the tyres.

'By the time he left the tarmac the deceleration had fallen to 1.3G.'

He was onto the run-off area, a broad arc of gravel. The Ferrari buck-bounded across that.

'The average deceleration in the gravel trap was 1.1G.'

Roger Chapman, sitting with his wife Amanda in the Jonathan Palmer stand on the inside of the corner, was a typical spectator. 'Schumacher applied the brakes and just managed to miss the back end of Irvine. It happened right in front of us. Everyone stood up in the stand and cheered. That was the first thing. Everyone went *yeahhh!*

'But when he hit the tyres, the whole crowd just went deathly quiet. You could tell what people were thinking. *Christ this looks bad … looks like the same thing that happened to Ayrton Senna.* It was amazing how the crowd went from being elated that Schumacher had gone off the track on the first lap to everyone thinking it could be serious. Although we might not like the chap too much, we don't want to see him killed.'

Once the car was motionless Schumacher tried to lever himself out. 'It was not a nice experience,' he would say. 'I was very soon aware of the problem but the worst moment was when I tried to get out of the car and couldn't because my leg was stuck inside. I couldn't really see what kind of injury it was.'

Chapman says that by now the crowd was very subdued. 'They realised that although he hadn't been killed outright, there was still the possibility of serious injury.'

Marshals were at the car and so was Professor Sid Watkins, Formula 1's resident doctor, who'd give his arrival time as 85 seconds. Watkins found Schumacher 'completely rational and totally himself' and was impressed by what he described as Schumacher's 'whole demeanour and his politeness … he was very, very cool.'

'Hello Sid, it's just my leg,' Schumacher said, 'it's not a big problem.' He asked Watkins to telephone his wife Corinna when he could to reassure her he'd suffered no more than a broken right leg – awkward since Watkins didn't know the number. He also asked that word be passed urgently to Todt to check Irvine's car because *I've had brake failure.*

'They came along with a big sheet which they normally put up to screen the driver off,' Chapman says. 'Everyone was

The San Marino Grand Prix at Imola, and guess who won? (Formula One Pictures)

very concerned. As with Senna, nobody knew how serious the situation was. It wasn't until he was actually on the stretcher and then sat up that everyone said, *well he seems to be OK*. Then the atmosphere became much more normal.'

The request to ring home was resolved when Schumacher reached the track's medical centre, because someone handed him a mobile phone. Within the hour his condition had been assessed and he was carried carefully to the helicopter which took him to Northampton General Hospital.

That late afternoon, at the end of the re-started race (Coulthard won, Hakkinen out with a rear wheel problem), Ferrari issued a statement in which Todt said: 'Michael Schumacher had an accident on the opening lap because of a problem with the rear brakes. We are investigating the cause. Michael has broken the tibia and fibula of the right leg. He is currently undergoing an operation in Northampton General Hospital.'

No driver had practised so much self denial for so long

Surgeons inserted a 30cm steel pin in the leg and no complications were envisaged.

Two days later Ferrari issued a statement explaining that they were 'conducting a full and urgent investigation. What has been established so far is that the accident was caused by a sudden loss of pressure of the rear brake circuit. This was due to the loosening of a brake bleed nipple on the left rear caliper. The reason for this loosening of the nipple has not yet been established. This component had been checked as part of the Saturday evening race preparation and there had been no subsequent servicing of that part. The data shows no problem either in the warm-up or indeed in the braking manoeuvres for the first half lap of the race. Ferrari will continue to try to establish the reasons for this failure.'

Schumacher was flown to Switzerland, where he now lived, and as his recovery began in a clinic there, the talk was of him being out for three months. Some silly stuff floated about, like the German newspaper which claimed that Ferrari would modify the cockpit so he could drive without using his right foot. It drew a lofty riposte from Brawn: 'This suggestion has not come from us. It has no foundation whatsoever.' Nor does the newspaper seem to have considered that at some point Professor Watkins, for so long a zealous guardian of each driver's well-being, might possibly have been invited to sanction a driver competing with his leg in plaster …

There'd be endless shifting speculation but amidst it all a great truth emerged. Ferrari had sculptured the task of finding Scheckter's successor with exquisite care. They'd hired the best driver and paid him more than any driver had ever been paid. They already had Stepney, who's forgotten more about motorsport than most people know. They'd hired Todt, a man of enormous and proven pedigree; and Brawn the clairvoyant; and Byrne who was as good as they come. They'd hired a number 2 for Schumacher – Irvine – whose contract was so constricting that it might have violated European conventions on human rights. Irvine's role was to cause no trouble, exhibit absolute obedience and garner points for the team wherever he could. That is what he had done. He had the biggest yacht in the harbour at Monte Carlo and in the circumstances he'd earned it because no driver in the history of modern grand prix racing – *none* – had practised so much self-denial for so long.

Since Scheckter won the title in 1979, Ferrari must have spent, allowing for inflation, some $2 *billion* dollars trying to continue the sacred dynasty. They'd had tragic Villeneuve and Pironi who betrayed the trust, feisty Arnoux and immaculate Prost, they'd gloried in *Il Leone* and his claws; they'd had voluble Alesi and patient Alboreto and Berger's ready, boyish smile. Now, without warning or preparation, the dynasty was being entrusted to a broth of a boy from Conlig in County Down who'd won a single F1 race, Melbourne, and that only because Schumacher couldn't win it. Irvine, second in the British Grand Prix, stood only 8 points behind Hakkinen.

Schumacher's crash opened up a role reversal so outrageously improbable as to seem a flight of fancy. It even seemed possible in those early speculation-laden days that somewhere in the final half of the season Michael Schumacher might find himself under the constriction of team orders which demanded *help Irvine win the Championship*.

'By Silverstone we were on the pace, we were *there*, no doubt about that,' Rory Byrne says. 'We were reasonably ahead in the Constructors' and contending strongly in the Drivers'. It was looking to be another exciting cliff-hanger of a season, us and McLaren virtually on par. Then of course we had the dreadful accident, and losing a key member of the team, who is also your number 1 driver, affects the overall performance.'

Had there been a feeling that 1999 could be the year?

'Oh yes, very much so. It was a quiet feeling: this time we can do it. Certainly we felt we could.'

Kate Moss looking stunned rather than stunning at Monaco. (Formula One Pictures)

And the car?

'Once we got to Imola we'd sorted out how to set it up, we had a reasonable development programme and it was looking good. There was a feeling of quiet confidence. You should never *say* you're confident of winning a Championship, because McLaren are formidable. Relatively speaking they're probably strong now like they were in the late-80s when they won 15 out of 16 races. You can never be complacent with them around, never start thinking *oh we'll just win* but I felt we were competing on pretty equal terms.'

Stepney, speaking after the Italian Grand Prix in September, takes up the story. 'Eddie has been one of the closest drivers [in terms of performance] that Michael has had, and that's been an important factor for us in continuing after the accident. OK, we haven't the same momentum that we had and McLaren have made a lot of mistakes, but everybody makes those.'

A complete dimension of that season's racing was taken away

He evaluates from the inside. 'If you look back over a season you have to see where your performances were. When you win races it's good, it's fantastic but, at the end of the day, you have to see what your performance would have been like *if McLaren had finished*. Look at most of the races. We'd probably have won about two on merit, Canada and Monte Carlo. The rest? We've been struggling and you have to put that into it although, OK, we're doing well and we've done well. We've done good races when McLaren have done bad races and vice versa …'

At Silverstone a complete dimension of that season's racing was taken away. There would be no more sleight-of-hand races which left everyone down the pit lane bemused, no more breath-taking mid-race sprints, no more redefining the art of the possible. This brings Stepney back to the eggs and the basket. 'It's a fact of life that people follow the greats, but you have to make sure you don't get drawn in to the point where you rely on them too much.'

And the dimension taken away? Stepney explores that, and in doing so explains the constrictions the modern driver like Schumacher lives with. 'I compare him with Senna, because that's the only comparison at that sort of level. I worked closely with Senna at Lotus, probably more closely than with Michael. The drivers seem to have gone further away, or I've gone further away, or they've been taken further away. I don't know which. Years ago you'd be a lot closer to them and spent a lot more time with them.

'Personally, I'd say Senna was a deeper thinker than Michael and a lot more aware of what was going on. That's not a criticism, it's just the way it is. Also this is a different era – not just a different era but with different technologies and that's the hardest thing to get into perspective.

'For example, these days everybody's talking about overtaking. Years ago you could overtake on skill and that's why Senna wanted electronic aids banned because you wouldn't have the difference between top line drivers and the others. When you give someone full electronic aids he can drive the car just like anybody else. You don't get the gear change mistakes like you used to – miss a gear and you'd be overtaken. With the electronic aids it's nearly impossible to miss a gear change. The machine won't let you.

'It means you drive to the limit, you're always on the limit, so how do people overtake you? You're on the brakes, on the limit, and everything is so close. How much overtaking did you see at Monza? Only Barrichello, who overtook two. Look at Barcelona. We were stuck behind Villeneuve, we had a car a second faster and we couldn't get past him. You can't push the cars to go past anymore but the drivers that are best always find a way past, always. You know immediately who can pass and who can't. The best ones think it through, throw the car – and they've done it. Senna was like that in the wet and so is Michael, both the same. They'd think ahead and place the car where they knew the other car wouldn't be. They'd be on a different line and at a different point.'

And they'd done it.

That's what had been borne away for ever on a stretcher at Imola, 1 May 1994, and what had been taken away on a stretcher at Silverstone, 11 July 1999.

The days, weeks and months which followed were a kaleidoscope of hard fact and colourful fiction. Schumacher became a saga. There was something almost hypnotic about watching the episodes play themselves out. Subtly strong forces constantly – and unexpectedly – pulled at these episodes. This, in chronological order, is the saga with all the twists and turns along the way and, as they say in the theatre, noises off, too.

Tuesday 13 July. Ferrari statement. 'Ferrari announces that it has reached an agreement with driver Mika Salo for the current Championship, to drive Ferrari car n. 3 [sic] starting from the Austrian GP.'

Thursday 15 July. Willi Weber visited Schumacher in the Swiss clinic and estimated he'd be out for three months. 'The most important thing is for him to become fully fit and recover from his leg injury properly,' Weber said. 'For those reasons a pause of three months seems realistic. He will need that long for a full recovery. We don't want to take any risks and the doctors have advised him not to. He doesn't want to come back too early and risk long-term sequels.' Weber would not be drawn on whether the injury might end Schumacher's career.

Monday 19 July. Schumacher left the clinic and went home to Geneva.

Tuesday 20 July. Schumacher gave his first interview since the crash, spoke of his feelings and actions as the Ferrari's brake locked, and said emphatically that talk of returning for the German Grand Prix on 1 August was 'complete nonsense. Unfortunately I don't have a turbo-charger to make my bones heal more quickly. My primary goal is to make a full recovery however long it takes. Then we'll see what happens next.'

Friday 23 July. In practice for the **Austrian** Grand Prix Irvine was ninth, Salo sixteenth.

Monaco – and guess who won? (Formula One Pictures)

Saturday 24 July. Irvine qualified third, the McLarens in front of him, Salo seventh. 'The gap is not so big,' Irvine said.

Sunday 25 July. Irvine drove a lovely tactical race to win, which prompted *Autosport* magazine to run a screamer across its front page.

WHO NEEDS SCHUEY?

Salo was ninth, admitting to a couple of mistakes. 'I am not happy with my result.' Irvine, disarmingly honest, accepted that this first race as team leader was 'very difficult because the expectations are so high.' Without Schumacher, he'd add, you lacked a point of reference for your own performance. 'I miss that comparison.'

I will work for the team and drive for Irvine – I could live with that

Friday 30 July. At Hockenheim for the **German** Grand Prix, Bernie Ecclestone suggested that if Schumacher couldn't drive at his own high level when he was fit again he'd retire. Schumacher, Ecclestone added, 'is always on his personal limit and, if he could not be, I believe he would rather stop.' Weber put his return at 12 to 16 weeks hence: 'Michael has not made the step forward we would have expected.' In practice Irvine was second and Salo seventh.

Saturday 31 July. Salo qualified fourth and Irvine fifth. Schumacher was interviewed on television in the garden of his Geneva home. He sat on a wicker garden seat, wearing a red Ferrari-Marlboro sweat shirt and white trousers, right leg stretched out. He was asked about life without racing. 'Obviously you wish to be on the circuit and not sitting at home. Basically I am pretty happy to sit here and give interviews and I'd like to say thanks to all my English supporters. I've had many, many nice letters and presents.' He was asked when he'd be back. 'That's a difficult question. Every week we have a meeting with the doctors but it's not only a bone problem, it's also on my heel.' He'd suffered a deep cut to the heel, something unpublicised after the crash. 'That's

affecting me more, because of the flexibility of my foot and I am not able to predict when things will be right.'

Sunday 1 August. Fifteen minutes before the start Schumacher spoke to the home fans via the giant video screens at the track. Salo led the race after Hakkinen had problems and – in a role reversal that Irvine found uncomfortable – dutifully moved aside so that the Ulsterman could win it. 'Once I had passed Mika [Salo] I knew I was safe, but Ross Brawn told me to speed up a bit.' Irvine now led the World Championship with 52 points, Hakkinen 44, and the church bells were rung in Maranello.

Monday 2 August. Schumacher was asked by German sports news agency SID whether he'd support Irvine when he did come back? 'If that's the case' – Irvine going for the Championship – 'I will work for the team and drive for Irvine. I could live with this situation because Eddie has driven often enough for me. Why shouldn't one pay that back? Even if one might not want to do it, that's life.' Schumacher conceded that his recovery was taking longer than expected and 'to be quite honest I don't have all that much hope anymore as far as the Championship is concerned. I still have not started my conditioning programme.'

Tuesday 3 August. Weber said that Schumacher might be driving again by the weekend if doctors gave him permission. 'If there are no objections or misgivings on the medical front, Michael will test on Saturday.' The idea was that Schumacher would be examined by doctors at Fiorano, then test there. Weber added that if Schumacher emerged from the driving 'fairly trouble-free' they'd have to think about Hungary on 15 August.

Wednesday 4 August. Schumacher's press officer, Heiner Buchinger, said: 'The heel

You're not meant to drink it, you're meant to spray it all over Monte Carlo. (Formula One Pictures)

OVERLEAF: *Silverstone, Stowe corner, lap one, 11 July.* (Formula One Pictures)

is still swollen and at the moment he is not able to move it as freely as he should. When I left him on Sunday he was still on crutches but Ferrari have prepared the test for Saturday. I have to say it is very unlikely he will be able to make that.' The medical would now be on the Friday, in Switzerland. 'We believe the chances of him being allowed to drive are slim, perhaps only five per cent, but he is keen to be back at the wheel as soon as possible. Of course he must also satisfy the regulation which insists that he is able to get out of the car in just five seconds, and there will be no special privileges for Michael.'

Thursday 5 August. Irvine denied reports that he was leaving Ferrari for the Stewart team in 2000 but rumours suggested he would, especially since di Montezemolo stated publicly that Schumacher would remain as No 1.

Friday 6 August. Ferrari statement. 'Today at 7pm Michael Schumacher visited his doctors. The check-up was sched- uled on the 19th of July when he left the Swiss clinic and returned home. The clinical evolution is very good at this time, but it is too early for him to return to F1 racing in the coming weeks. In order to improve bone healing the consultant surgeons have decided to perform a partial hardware removal of the distal tibia. The rehabilitation programme will start again on the day after surgery. This might allow Michael Schumacher to make his comeback at Monza.' However, even if he did compete in the Italian Grand Prix on 12 September, his Championship chances were now essentially over.

Monday 9 August. Di Montezemolo went a long way to confirming the Schumacher/Irvine role reversal by insisting that 'the day Schumacher gets back it will be to help Ferrari. There's no doubt about it. What we care about is Ferrari's victory.' Di Montezemolo reiterated that by Monza Schumacher would 'have no

... and grand dad Rolf (Action Press/Rex Features)

chance to contend for the title. Drivers must follow directives. Schumacher has said it and he will do it: he'll be at Ferrari's service.'

Friday 13 August. In practice for the **Hungarian** Grand Prix Irvine was quickest and Salo fifth.

Saturday 14 August. Irvine qualified second – 'I had thought that if I could get pole anywhere it would be here' – and Salo eighteenth.

Sunday 15 August. Irvine finished third after losing control of the car on lap 63 and running wide. Salo, twelfth and two laps down, had a 'terrible race.' Hakkinen won, making it Irvine 56, Hakkinen 54. Schumacher was reported to be working in the gym up to eight hours a day to maintain his fitness.

It was like coming home after a too-long holiday

Wednesday 18 August. Salo tested at Fiorano and did 63 laps working mainly on the set-up of the car. Ferrari announced that next day Schumacher would 'undergo another medical examination to check on the course of his condition.'

Thursday 19 August. Ferrari statement. 'Today at 7pm Michael Schumacher underwent a further medical examination. This check-up had been planned at the time of his previous examination on 6th August. The outcome of the check-up showed that his physical conditions were positive, and the next step will be to drive a few laps of the Mugello circuit at the wheel of an F399. This test will be carried out tomorrow.'

Friday 20 August. Schumacher was flown to Mugello by helicopter.

Ferrari statement that evening:

Circuit: Autodromo del Mugello, 5.20 Km
Driver: Eddie Irvine, F399, chassis number 193;
           Michael Schumacher, Mika Salo, F399, chassis number 194.
Weather: Air Temp. 22–30C, Track, 32–50C, sunny.

Testing began on the dot at 09h30. Mika Salo did just one shake-down lap in car 194. Eddie Irvine continued his programme of working on set-up and adjustments in preparation for the forthcoming Belgian Grand Prix. Michael Schumacher's testing went smoothly with a series of runs of about five laps each, followed by one 20-lap run. Today was Ferrari's last day of testing at Mugello.

Michael Schumacher	1.28.379	65 laps
Eddie Irvine	1.28.648	59 laps

Jean Todt: 'It was great to have the whole group together, with Eddie and Mika when Michael arrived [sic]. I had expected Michael to only do a handful of laps but in the end he managed to do a whole day's testing. The two drivers worked on different programmes, with Eddie preparing for the Belgian Grand Prix and Michael reacquainting himself with the car in race trim. I had thought Michael could be back for Monza. We will see how he feels after this test and make a decision after a further medical examination. Tomorrow, at Fiorano, Mika Salo will shake down the three cars to be used in next week's Belgian Grand Prix.'

Eddie Irvine: 'I worked mainly in preparation for the race at Spa. Today, I concentrated on brakes, which still give me a few problems to adjust correctly. I did all my laps today in race trim'

Michael Schumacher: 'Above all, I want to thank all the Ferrari fans. Today, I was very happy with the reception I got from the team and it was great to see my friends again. It was like coming home after a too-long holiday. Almost straight away I felt comfortable with the car, although it took me a short while to adapt to the change of balance of the car. I did around 60 laps without any problems. Over the bumps, my right leg hurt a bit, but it had no effect on my performance. Over the next few days I will see how I feel and, after a further medical check, I will decide along with the team if I can make my comeback at Monza or earlier.'

Such statements are neat summaries but dry. You'd scarcely deduce from this that Schumacher had shaken Formula 1 with what was a sensational performance.

Mugello is not the easiest of tracks, he had a pronounced limp, yet his first proper lap was within a whisker of the best time Irvine had managed thus far in the day – and then Schumacher finished the day 0.3 of a second quicker.

Monday 23 August. Schumacher went cycling, a good test of his leg, and was in pain afterwards.

Tuesday 24 August. Ferrari statement. 'Eddie Irvine and Mika Salo will drive in the Belgian Grand Prix on 29th August. Michael Schumacher will drive the following week at Monza during tests for the Italian GP. At the test, which will run from the first to third September, he will carry out a race distance simulation as preparation for a possible participation in the Italian GP.'

Thursday 26 August. At Spa for the **Belgian** Grand Prix, Irvine said: 'I assume that as I'm going for the Championship and I am leading at the minute Ferrari will want to back me. At the start of the year Michael was the best chance the team had and it was logical to back him. Things have changed now. I've scored 30 points in four races. But it is Jean Todt's decision – I haven't asked. I work for the team and do what I'm told to do.'

Friday 27 August. Salo was eighth and Irvine ninth in free practice.

Saturday 28 August. Irvine qualified sixth and Salo ninth. 'The car is simply not quick enough,' Irvine said.

Sunday 29 August. Irvine finished the race fourth and Salo seventh. 'Considering our situation today,' Irvine said, 'I am happy that I am only one point behind the new leader in the Championship.' Coulthard won from Hakkinen, giving: Hakkinen 60, Irvine 59, Coulthard 46, Frentzen 40.

Tuesday 31 August. Irvine said he believed Schumacher would return for the Italian Grand Prix. 'I have no reason to believe he is not coming back to help me.'

The decisive test session at Mugello before he decided to come back. (Formula One Pictures)

Wednesday 1 September. General testing at Monza. Ferrari statement. 'Testing began at 09h00. During the morning the drivers concentrated on setting up their cars. Irvine managed only a few laps before the lunch break, because of a problem with the hydraulic system. In the afternoon each driver worked on a different programme, all of them as part of the preparation for next week's Italian GP. Michael Schumacher's programme also ended prematurely, because of an hydraulic problem. Testing ended at 18h30.'

Several hundred *tifosi* were in the stand opposite the pits – where so long ago Scheckter had passed on his way to the finishing line – and they draped their banners, several in English.

SCHUMY YOU ARE MAGIC
WELCOME BACK SCHUMI
WE MISSED YOU MICHAEL

One was in Italian and requires no translation

MAGICO SCHUMY!

Schumacher said: 'I made a test today and the problems in my leg are too big to do a proper job. It is basically impossible for me to run more than five laps at the moment and especially on this circuit. The bumps and curves are pretty severe. It is pretty difficult. I had pain all the way through and you can't drive like that. I took painkillers but it didn't really help. I don't think I will compete in the next two races. After the surgery the doctor said I would not be back in the car for 12 to 16 weeks. Here I am after seven weeks. Maybe you can say it was too early, but we had to try. It is not a step back – we just must take more time. We will stop the testing today, consolidate and I will have a meeting with my doctors on Sunday.'

He was asked if he was delaying his return to avoid having to help Irvine. 'I and Eddie Irvine have always driven for Ferrari. I don't believe Eddie ever drove for me and my interest, and I wouldn't drive for him. We drive for the team.' It is,

> I don't believe Eddie ever drove for my interests and I wouldn't for his

perhaps, a nice play on words compared to what he'd said on 2 August, but never mind.

Thursday 2 September. Schumacher didn't test but Irvine and Salo did.

Friday 3 September. The last day of the test: Irvine went quickest (1:23.927) from Coulthard (1:24.299), Salo fourth.

Saturday 4 September. Ferrari statement. 'Ferrari hereby announces that the driver Rubens Barrichello has been signed to drive for Scuderia Ferrari-Marlboro for the next two seasons alongside Michael Schumacher. Ferrari wishes to thank Eddie Irvine for his constructive and loyal collaboration with the team over the past four seasons. Both the team and the driver will put all their efforts and determination into tackling the decisive four remaining races of the Championship.'

Monday 6 September. Heiner Buchinger said: 'The situation has not changed. The recovery process is taking place normally. Sadly, it is not going any quicker than expected.' This meant Schumacher would miss the European Grand Prix at the Nürburgring on 26 September.

Friday 10 September. Irvine was 16th and Salo 17th in practice for the **Italian** Grand Prix at Monza.

Saturday 11 September. Salo qualified sixth and Irvine eighth.

Sunday 12 September. Salo finished the race third and Irvine sixth – Hakkinen crashed. That made Irvine and Hakkinen joint leaders of the championship on 60 points.

Tuesday 14 September to Thursday 16 September. Irvine and Salo tested at Mugello.

Friday 17 September. Test driver Luca Badoer did 59 laps at Fiorano, making final adjustments to the F399 in preparation for the Nürburgring.

Saturday 18 September. Irvine 'shook down' the three cars which would be taken to the Nürburgring. 'In the late afternoon,' Ferrari said, 'he also carried out some rain tyre tests after the track had been artificially flooded.'

Monday 20 September. Buchinger revealed that Schumacher would drive at

Fiorano on 7 October. 'Michael will definitely be at Fiorano,' Buchinger said, adding that he wanted to compete in the last two races of the season.

Tuesday 21 September. The new Jaguar Formula 1 car (nee Stewart) was unveiled at the Frankfurt Motor Show and Irvine was confirmed as the man to partner Herbert in 2000.

Thursday 23 September. Schumacher gave an interview to RTL. 'Ferrari will only win if McLaren keep making mistakes and give it away. For this race and for the Championship McLaren have improved their car and they are in better shape than Ferrari. I think that it is not going to be Eddie's year. Only bad luck can stop Mika beating him and the only way Ferrari will finish with a Championship is if McLaren give it to them.' Schumacher added: 'Malaysia is still the target but at the moment I cannot be sure about that. We have to see what happens when I drive the car again. I am training but I am still not 100 per cent fit. I have to be guided by the doctors. There will be no point in taking unnecessary risks.' This interview, variously described as an outburst and the perfect model of bad timing, exploded all around Irvine amid a riot of headlines.

WOUNDED IRVINE

SCHUMACHER DISMISSES IRVINE TITLE BID

and so on, in similar vein.

This interview gave ammunition to those who believed Schumacher didn't want Irvine to be the driver to give Ferrari the longed-for Championship and didn't intend to ride shotgun to help him do so. Schumacher could avoid any such dilemma by not racing, and his medical condition allowed that.

The Agnelli dynasty keeping a paternal eye on Ferrari and the people working for it. (Formula One Pictures)

It was a dilemma that probed deeply into what manner of man Schumacher really was. A strong body of opinion believed he could never bring himself to help Irvine; an equally strong body believed that if he did help (even reluctantly) it would transform his global image from the implacable machine we had seen so often into a misunderstood, rounded human being. Some believed he would help Irvine *because* he was misunderstood. All were agreed, however, that if Schumacher risked aggravating the injury he'd be crazy to race whatever the circumstances. For the moment it rested there.

Deep in the background, though, there lurked a notion that Ferrari did not want Irvine to win the crown either. The supposed logic here was that, having invested so totally in Schumacher, Ferrari would look foolish if the subservient No 2 achieved it instead. Not surprisingly Ferrari vehemently denied this.

Grand prix racing, we know, is tightly packed with conspiracy theorists obsessively wringing complexity out of simplicity; and further, that in its most virulent form there are conspiracy theorists trying to work out how many conspiracy theorists are at work within Ferrari.

By now, the saga was so multi-faceted that the wringing became wonderful to behold.

However, the notion that Ferrari would have spent their annual $200 million in 1999 *not* to have a World Champion, to deliberately deprive themselves of the Championship after 20 years of struggle for it, seemed quite mad. No wonder they issued the vehement denials. More than that, they proved conclusively by their actions at the end of the season how mad the notion had been.

Friday 24 September. In practice for the **European** Grand Prix, Irvine was fourth and Salo second. That of course wasn't the story flooding out from the Nürburgring. Irvine, caught at the very heart of the fallout from the Schumacher-RTL explosion, insisted that 'what Michael says is not important. What matters is what happens on the track here on Sunday. All I can say

is that he obviously has less faith in Ferrari than I do.'

Saturday 25 September. Irvine qualified ninth and Salo twelfth. 'A poor result,' Irvine said, 'but we have not given up.'

Sunday 26 September. Irvine finished the race seventh and Salo retired on lap 45. Todt described it thus: 'The race was a series of problems enlivened with much drama,' and you could certainly put it like that. Irvine, for example, arrived for a pit stop to discover 'they could not find one of my tyres.' In fact Salo had just been in to change a damaged front wing and this confused everything. 'The pit crew was ready for me,' Irvine explained, 'but Salo came in first and so the mechanics got rid of my tyres to put his tyres on.' Hakkinen 62 points, Irvine 60, Frentzen 50, Coulthard 48.

The conspiracy theorists went to work like carnivores on the image of a mechanic by Irvine's rear wheel with no tyre in his hands, as if somehow here was proof that Ferrari didn't want Irvine to win. There are many, many refined and invisible methods of nobbling a racing car, if that is what you want. One of those methods is *not* to do it in the most public, risible and childishly obvious way: a mechanic exactly framed on several hundred million television screens all over the world, standing empty-handed.

Back at Maranello after the race di Montezemolo banished all notions of this nonsense and proved Ferrari's sincerity by calling a crisis meeting with leading team members. It lasted some two and a half hours and he emerged to say: 'we can still win the Championship. It's not over.'

Tuesday 28 September. Badoer tested at Fiorano, covering 83 laps.

Wednesday 29 September – Thursday 30 September. Salo tested at Fiorano.

Friday 1 October – Saturday 2 October. Irvine tested at Mugello preparing for the Malaysian Grand Prix. He worked on the engine and aerodynamics then did a simulated race distance.

Sunday 3 October. Ferrari statement. 'This afternoon Michael Schumacher underwent a medical examination in

Paris. This showed that the bones have healed sufficiently for him to resume normal activities. Tomorrow, Schumacher will drive an F399 at the Mugello circuit for a series of shake-downs. Michael Schumacher has informed Ferrari of his decision not to take part in the remaining two grands prix of the season, as he feels he is not sufficiently fit to cope with the demands of a race.'

Monday 4 October. Ferrari statement from Mugello. 'Testing began at 10h00. At first, Michael Schumacher worked on the set-up of his car, then he worked on checking and shaking down a few mechanical components. He did a total of 69 laps with a best time of 1m 27.287. Testing ended at 18h30. This was the final day of testing at Mugello.'

The statement did not mention that Schumacher had spun off after about 15 laps, kissing a barrier and inflicting light damage on the car. He walked away unaided and continued in another car – but did say he'd been frightened. 'My mind went back to certain bad things. It's not nice to be scared in that moment.'

Sections of the German press rounded on him for his decision not to race, using strong language. One newspaper hammered out question after question in what they termed as the SCHUMI PUZZLE, while another spoke in the language of egomania and reprimanded him for showing 'no hint of a sense of duty' to Ferrari – who'd made him the highest-paid driver ever..

Tuesday 5 October – Wednesday 6 October. Irvine tested at Fiorano.

Thursday 7 October. Schumacher joined Irvine in the testing. Ferrari said that 'at the end of the morning' Irvine did 'a few runs to check and adjust settings on the test car. At the beginning of the afternoon Michael Schumacher drove the same car, carrying out tyre tests over a distance of 58 laps.'

Friday 8 October. Ferrari statement. 'Testing began at 09h30. This morning, Michael Schumacher worked on set-up and tyre testing with the F399. He did a total of 34 laps with a best time of

1m 00.942. In the afternoon, the track was artificially flooded and Michael did 43 laps.' That 1:00.942 was fast.

Some hours later …

'Ferrari announces that Michael Schumacher will take part in the Malaysian and Japanese Grands Prix. After 3 days of intensive testing at Mugello and Fiorano, Michael saw that there had been a big improvement in his physical condition and therefore he has decided to take part in the two final and very important races of the season, to give the maximum support to Ferrari in the fight for the Championships and to fulfil the wishes of the team and all the fans.'

Saturday 9 October. 'The belief that I'd be able to make it has grown bit by bit over the last few days,' Schumacher said. 'What was important was seeing how much the team wanted me to be there. I'm not at 100 per cent but I've realised that I have to be there. Obviously I too wanted to make this comeback but I had to convince myself – and these practice sessions, first at Mugello then at Fiorano, gave me the confirmation. And then there was also the desire to help the team and to help Eddie.' Schumacher insisted that 'when I made it known that I wouldn't be in a condition to race I wasn't bluffing. I felt good, but it's one thing to go for a walk in the park and it's another to endure a grand prix.'

There can be no doubt that Ferrari had missed Schumacher, if only for his analytical input; no doubt that Irvine missed Schumacher to intimidate Hakkinen psychologically and bring his full range of talents to helping the cause; little doubt that Irvine implored di Montezemolo to try to persuade Schumacher to drive in Malaysia and Japan.

And he'd said yes.

By Silverstone he had become very tired and nervous, which is not like him

OVERLEAF: *Maestro. Schumacher returns in Malaysia and controls the whole race, passing the lead to Irvine twice.* (Formula One Pictures)

145

Later, differing versions emerged of what happened next. Before the final test Corinna expressed 'strong reservations' about his coming back. However, said Schumacher, 'when she saw me come back home after the last test at Mugello, she reacted intelligently. For the first time in a long time she saw a smile on my face.' Di Montezemolo insisted he had ordered Schumacher back and recounted how he'd telephoned but Schumacher's daughter, Gina-Maria, had answered and said 'daddy was getting out his football boots.' Di Montezemolo concluded that if Schumacher could play football he could drive the Ferrari; and would.

Schumacher explained he'd met di Montezemolo although 'I think I'm independent enough to make my own decisions. I discussed my feelings and reservations. I explained why I said no, and why I said yes.'

And he'd said yes. Ultimately it was as simple as that – again.

Long before Malaysia, Nigel Stepney said: 'I think that when Michael comes back he's going to be stronger – stronger mentally because drivers get tired and they don't realise it. Sometimes it's better to walk away and leave it for a couple of weeks. When you come back you feel better and you work better. At the point of the Silverstone accident he had reached saturation. He was very tired and started to get very nervous, which is not like him, but he wanted the Championship this year, you could see he *wanted* it. OK, he'd got close in 1997 and 1998 but close is still a long way away. There is a lot more to come. His motivation is still to want to win.'

Nor was the Ferrari designer Rory Byrne remotely surprised that Schumacher could reach real racing pace immediately. 'A typical example was the test he did at Mugello after his accident when he hadn't driven a car for a couple of months or whatever it was. We'd had Mika Salo and Eddie testing for a couple of days and Michael got in. Nothing special done to the car, proper fuel load, standard tyres, no tricks, and on his very first run of the day he put in a faster lap than either Mika or Eddie had done in the last two. Straight away, just *bomp*, just like that.'

In Stepney's judgement it goes beyond driving. 'Nobody can handle the overall situation at Ferrari better than him. I don't think there is another driver in Formula 1 at the moment who could.

'Senna had such a big following and people loved him but it wasn't just for his driving. They came to see *him* because they knew he was magic and there was always going to be something happening, something special. That's true of Schumacher as well, although it's a different following because South American people are a lot warmer than the following of Schumacher.'

In **Malaysia** Schumacher had to prove he was fit enough to get out of the cockpit in less than five seconds, an essential precaution in case of accidents. He did. Professor Watkins said 'he is in perfect and sound health. He did a little hop for us' – a reference to one of Watkins' tests for complete recovery of a leg injury: prove to us you can jump up and down on it.

Schumacher said he thought he could win the race but 'my fitness is not as it was before.' Of Irvine he said: 'I must make it clear that I am first of all driving for the team and not in the interests of Eddie. The only way I can help him is to be in front and let him past. If that is not the case he will have to manage on his own.'

On the Friday Irvine was fourth and Schumacher fifth. 'I am glad to say I felt absolutely no pain and so I was able to concentrate fully on the driving. The car is fun to drive on this circuit.' On the Saturday he took pole and was stunning.

Schumacher	1:39.688
Irvine	1:40.635
Coulthard	1:40.806
Hakkinen	1:40.866

'I expected we would be strong here,' Schumacher said, 'but to be one second ahead is surprising. I only did eight laps as I could see my time would not be beaten and I wanted to keep as many tyres as possible to have greater flexibility in the race. As for the race, I plan to go flat out to the finish, then we will see what the positions are. Of course if I am in front at the end with Eddie behind me I will let him through.'

In the race Schumacher led, waved Irvine through and although Coulthard overtook him – 'that was not part of the plan' – he kept Hakkinen behind. Towards the end, Coulthard out with a fuel pressure problem, Schumacher led again and let Irvine through again. An impression of that race: Schumacher controlling cars in front *and* behind, shaping the whole race, deciding who was doing what. Brundle, commentating on television, caught that nicely: *Schumacher has spent the afternoon going as slowly as possible and he's still had to give the lead away twice …*

There remained the controversy over the Ferrari's bargeboards – aerodynamic 'fins' on the flanks of the cars aiding airflow and stability – which were found to be a fraction too small on their bottom edges. This led to the exclusion of the cars and made Hakkinen World Champion pending Ferrari's appeal, heard in Paris the week after the race. The appeal was upheld and opened up the Championship again. That Championship lay devalued because the best driver in the world was not in contention for it. At Malaysia Schumacher had been operating on a plateau no competitor could reach or perhaps *imagine* reaching.

Had it finally led to communion?

For many years Pino Allievi has been the motor racing correspondent of the Italian daily *La Gazzetta dello Sport*. He is inevitably steeped in Ferrari lore and is an

The Malaysian podium, Irvine circumspect – but now with the world to win – and Hakkinen cast down. (Formula One Pictures)

absolute authority on the team. Speaking to the author in 1999 he said: 'Schumacher is like a cyber-pilot. Italians respect him but they love people who have something to transmit from the heart – he speaks in Press Releases.

'Italians are indifferent to him. Ferrari is important to him because he is racing for Ferrari – it could just as easily be a team from Luxembourg or anywhere. Italians are not anti-German or anti-anybody. We've had German footballers like Haller, Muller and Bierhof, speaking very good Italian, and that was no problem. Look at Berger, a German speaker. Look at Niki Lauda, if you want to talk about Anglo-Saxons, and remember how much people felt for him. And Jody Scheckter – he was loved.'

Schumacher did not speak Italian, perhaps then for what appeared to be a good reason. The language of motor racing is English and really that's all you need. Yet what might even a few phrases in Italian mean to the *tifosi* yearning to know if emo-tionally he was one of them? The answer came, of course, at the 2001 launch. It meant a lot.

Schumacher unloved. Harsh? Maybe. True? Maybe. As someone said, it's a powerful hard thing pleasing all the people all of the time. You can doubtless find many thousand fans in Italy and across the globe who treasure Schumacher's bluntness, respect his *I'll speak my mind if I want*, adore his talents and see in him the ultimate modern sportsman: rich and confident, part businessman, part private individual, part technocrat, and all rendered a caricature by the monster of global celebrity. Nor is this something he can ever escape. It's why, in 'Straight from the grid', I described his trying to tweak Brundle's ear and swat Ralf's head. Those are the precious moments when he returns to a central part of himself: the lean lad from Kerpen of modest family means, the boy next door.

Otherwise, what you see is what you get, and what you get is a hell of a lot; and always a lot more coming.

Rainmaster. (Formula One Pictures)

chapter six

Brain, Brawn, and a horse to tame

That Sunday afternoon at Suzuka – 31 October 1999 – a Championship had been won, a Championship had been lost, and you could sense the Ferrari team being drawn into conflicting emotions. The Constructors' title is highly valued within Formula 1, and beating McLaren produced a vast smile on Nigel Stepney's face. But the Drivers' title is the one which gathers all the publicity, and Irvine so narrowly losing that to Hakkinen was hard to take.

Five years ago if Ferrari had achieved this it would have been regarded as a near miracle. The team had now hauled and lifted themselves to a level of expectation where there was open disappointment at winning 'only' one of those titles.

So what's the view from inside Ferrari? Ross Brawn, the Technical Director, talks candidly about life with Schumacher.

'It's a tribute to the team that they have got to the stage where finishing second in the Drivers' Championship two points behind the winner was a disaster. [SMALL, POLITE LAUGH] This could have been the third Drivers' Championship for Ferrari and it's frustrating from that point of view because we've got down to the last race in the last three years. I think the first year was treated as "well, great, we got this far and we should be proud of what we did", but the third time it does get a bit frustrating.'

Do you think it may be a slight problem motivating people for number 4?

'I don't think so, no. We won the Constructors' Championship, which was a boost for everyone. It's still a pretty big achievement. They vary their opinion to suit circumstance, but if you listen to Frank [Williams] and Ron [Dennis] they say the Constructors' is always more important to them than the Drivers'. In the circumstances we actually had a great season considering we lost Michael half way through and he was missing for six races. To win the Constructors' and finish second in the Drivers' is, as I keep telling everyone here, something that they should be proud of.'

Also it is reasonable to say Schumacher could have won it.

'I'd like to think so, yes. Hakkinen beat Eddie by two points at the end of the day and any comparison you make, that's a pretty poor performance from them and a pretty good performance from Eddie.'

When you went to Ferrari from Benetton for the 1997 season, was Schumacher instrumental? Did he want you or was this something Ferrari wanted?

'It was a mix really. The circumstances were that he and Ferrari had heard that I'd had one or two disappointments at Benetton – not Benetton directly but

[Flavio] Briatore had made some commitments to me to change the structure of the team because I felt we needed to reconsider that structure for the future. Although 1996 was pretty disastrous we were still competitive – we just didn't put it together, lost several races and so on. It was a particularly difficult year because of the new drivers [Alesi, Berger] and losing Michael. I became even more convinced that those changes were necessary but during 1996 Briatore didn't carry them out. At the same time Michael was having a bit of a difficult time [at Ferrari].'

John Barnard has described some of those difficulties.

Michael's aim is to win with Ferrari, that's his number one ambition

'I have to be honest. My time here at Ferrari with John was very good. I had no problem with John at all and he was very supportive. In the short period we had together I had no complaints at all.'

I think he felt that if you had been there from the start with Schumacher, and Barnard had been doing what he wanted to do from Guildford, it would have been the perfect arrangement – but he was being drawn back to the pit lane because they didn't have a Ross Brawn getting hold of it.

'Middle of 1996 Willi Weber was the first person to contact me and say "look, I hear some rumblings that things are not quite right at Benetton. If you do ever consider leaving would you contact us?" I gave it some thought and then got in contact with Willi and Jean Todt. It really went from there.'

There's nothing sinister about this. A man like Schumacher wants his own people around him and he will perform better.

'Yes.'

Can you please unlock the door to the famous tactics? I watch races like Hungary in 1998 and when it's over I don't know how it was done. Lots of people are thinking he couldn't have won that, could he – it's impossible.

'The thing that is important to stress is that Michael is a driver who takes a great deal of time to understand the tactical considerations and the tactical options during a race. He will spend a great deal of time, particularly on a Saturday evening, with me and the other members of the team to contribute to those tactical considerations. There are direct things he can contribute in terms of how easy it is to overtake here, which way does the track "go" during a race – does it pick up pace, does it stabilise etc? There's information from him that we need in order to be able to make a decision, but he's astute enough to throw in proposals: have you actually thought about this, have you thought about that, what happens if we do so-and-so?

'He understands the principles behind reaching a tactical decision and he contributes as well. His strength is that he spends that effort on a Saturday, and sometimes on a Sunday morning, then when he gets into the race he listens to what we want to do – because he knows his part now is to drive the car with an understanding of what we want to do. We never get a discussion during the race: we have confidence in him and he has confidence in us.'

So you don't discuss it then?

'Very rarely, it's very rare during a race that we discuss it in order to make a decision. We discuss it in the sense of "right Michael, this is what we are doing now, we're going to Plan B or Plan C and you understand what you've got to do."'

But what about when Ross Brawn says 'by the way we're going to Plan D, which I hadn't mentioned to you before, Michael'?

'We don't do that, unless we've had something crazy go on – because all of the things we do in a race have been considered beforehand. It's only if the race falls apart that you have to start doing a few things purely by intuition, and those races generally aren't the races you win, they are the races where you are trying to salvage some points.'

If you ask him to do the unexpected, can he do it?

The clairvoyant? Brawn and Schumacher at work. (Formula One Pictures)

152

'Well, it's not unexpected any more. That's a little bit of a contradiction because what he does know is what we expect him to do. You mentioned Hungary and his performance in the middle of the race. When we said "right Michael, this is what you've got to achieve" he just lit up. That's his talent.'

John Barnard explained that if you got on the phone to, for example, Berger and said 'look, we want you to go faster for a certain number of laps', he'd tell you where to go because he's already driving as fast as he can, whereas Schumacher says 'OK' and seems to be able to go to a kind of qualifying mode at will and come off it at will.

'Like every driver, I imagine, Michael drives at a certain percentage during a race because there is a risk involved if you drive at the maximum every lap, but he does have more ability than anyone to drive at 99.9 per cent of the car's limit for a long period. It was quite a shock to me when we had Jean and Gerhard join Benetton after having Michael, because when we got into the race we'd see a tactical opportunity and we'd say "right guys, this is it, now you've got a clear track, you've got to pull the pace up" and nothing happened. Sometimes Jean and Gerhard went slower because they were then trying too hard. We'd become accustomed to getting on the radio to Michael and saying "right, you've got to find some time now" and then you'd start to see the times coming up. It *was* quite a shock because that had become normal and it became abnormal when we lost Michael.'

What is this ability? Why can he do it and Senna could do it and others just can't?

'Well, the thing is the others are hanging in there by their finger nails. That's the reality. Some of the drivers are having to drive like that just to be respectable. Michael can drive a very respectable race with a lot of spare margin.'

Does he get excited in the race? Senna used to come on the radio and give them a hell of a time with the language and all the rest of it: part of his brain was shouting 'what's going on?' and the other part of his brain was very cold.

'Michael doesn't do that at all. The other remarkable thing about Michael is when we talk on the radio it's like you and I having this conversation, it's a perfectly normal discussion. He gets upset with other things that can happen in the race, like the incidents with Coulthard. Then you hear a different side of Michael on the radio that you never hear during the ordinary running of a race. What I like about Michael is that even the most aggressive tactics from other drivers in normal racing never solicit a comment from him. So if somebody does something to him in a race that I, from the outside, would think was a pretty audacious move he will just treat it as normal racing, nothing to be complaining about.'

… whereas with Coulthard in Suzuka he didn't feel it was normal racing, it was a deliberate attempt to obstruct him.

'In both Spa and Suzuka Coulthard was being lapped, and I think that's what upset Michael. Any comparisons with the tactical decisions that we made in Malaysia weren't valid because that was two drivers on the same lap racing for position.'

What did you make of Schumacher's race in Malaysia?

'It was astonishing.'

Even to you?

'Yes, a bit. I'd started to see it in testing because Jean [Todt] and I decided the best way to convince Michael to come back was to give him a good car and let him enjoy himself. So, in the testing at Fiorano and Mugello, our approach was to not put pressure on him – he was the only one who could make the decision whether he was ready to come back or not – but to make sure we gave him the maximum opportunity to enjoy himself.'

Which he did.

'We must always remember that these guys are doing it – or at least they began to do it – because they love motor racing.'

I think he still does.

'They all still do, absolutely. They get the fame and the fortune, and sometimes people forget that deep down they are racing drivers, they love racing, they love beating their competitors, they love making the car work. All those things are their real passion. People say, and it's true, that they earn all this money but certainly Michael's objective is to win with Ferrari, that's his number one ambition. So when we were able to put him in a car that was working very well – we'd been able to have a bit of a development programme on a couple of things that were very interesting – you could see his enthusiasm was enormous. By the end of that week, when we said "look Michael, it would really help us if you could join us for the last couple of races," it didn't take much to convince him. We knew he was in a really strong frame of mind.'

Everything about him suggested he was strong.

'Yes, he was A1.'

Watching that race, he was controlling what was happening in front of him, he was controlling what was happening behind him: it was like somebody conducting an orchestra.

'He always has spare mental capacity when he's driving a car. When some of the drivers are at the limit they've got nothing left mentally or physically. Michael, you always feel, has a margin – not to make the car go faster but to think about other things, and in a race like Malaysia he's perfect because he's taking everything into consideration.'

Are you born with that?

'I think a large percentage, yes. I mean, he is a very bright person and he has realised that he needs to maintain his physical fitness to a level where that's not even a consideration during a race. That was probably the only reason for his reluctance to come back too early: he knows the level he can perform at and he was very concerned that his physical fitness would distract from the way he knows he can race. It wasn't just a question of coming back and driving a car – because he knew he could do that – but competing and being at the front, where he wants to be. He needed to have that margin of physical fitness back at the level where it didn't encroach on his ability to drive a race or control a race. And it didn't. At that stage he had overcome his difficulties to the point where he could handle it.'

I could never see Schumacher, any more than I could ever see Senna, become a 30-something-year-old midfield runner. They'd have left it by then because they could no longer do it at their level, which is the highest level.

'You're right. There will be a point where Michael will decide that he can't do it the way he wants to do it, and that's what people didn't understand about his injury. It was nothing to do with him being physically capable of driving the car.'

He'll be able to do that when he's 55, be able to take one round.

'Yes! It was not being able to undertake the fitness regime, the training that he normally does in order to ensure that his fitness is not a consideration during the race.'

It's easy to concentrate on one man in a team.

'Championships are won by groups of people, not by an individual, and we have a very good group of people here – with Michael driving the car, obviously, Todt in charge …'

Todt has done an outstanding job and not been given the praise.

'It's a very unfortunate situation in that people don't understand what Todt does.'

I remember what it was like before he got there.

'Others have very short memories, therefore I think it's a tragedy that Jean is not given the credit for what he's done here and what he continues to do. It is a very unfortunate side of the media – they don't really understand. They draw opinion from outside and that opinion escalates like a snowball and sometimes there's no stopping it. I hope we can get both championships because it would be a tribute to Jean's work here. He has been very instrumental in putting everything together.'

What sort of a chap is Schumacher? This is a particularly English question because whatever he does some will see him as the archetypal

> **People who work with him have a great deal of passion for Michael**

German and I guess he has accepted that and said 'well, there's nothing I can do.'

'I think people who know him have at the very least a great deal of respect for him and most of the people who know him like him a great deal. If you talk to any of the people at Benetton they love Michael. They thought he was a great driver and he was great for the team and they all do have a huge respect. The people who work closely with him have a great deal of passion for Michael.'

Maybe it's those who've only seen him from a distance.

'I had an instance a couple of years ago. My accountant comes to the British Grand Prix on a Saturday and that Saturday evening he was in the garage with his wife and his son. The son was a huge Michael fan but his wife was one of the ones who perhaps believed the media image of him. I introduced them and Michael was his normal charming self. I had a letter from her a few days later: she was completely bowled over. She'd had the image of Michael being this vicious Kraut, she met him and it was totally the opposite. She confessed she was completely taken with him and that's the contrast: there's the media image and there's the real opinions of people who work with him.'

Senna once said 'I'm at the front the whole time and so the cameras are on me the whole time and everything I do is seen and dissected. If you are running at the back you can do all manner of things and people tend not to notice so much.' A bit the same with Schumacher?

'Yes, that's absolutely true. I find him a very genuine person. I mean, he's very ambitious and very strong and sometimes we disagree on things but it's never in a personal way. We have a professional disagreement about how something should be done or how it should be run but he's never machiavellian, he deals with things straight up in front. He's just very, very straight.'

Obviously both of you think the same way.

'Yes, the majority of times, yes.'

You're not telepathic or anything, are you? I've called you clairvoyant but telepathy on top of that would be too much.

[CHUCKLE]. 'No.'

When you get on the phone and say 'right, we're going to Plan B' does he say 'I knew you were going to say that, I've been waiting for you to ring'?

'No, he doesn't quite do that but there is, I guess, an empathy. I know he's going to do a job and hopefully he knows I am going to do a job: you know that together is the only way to go forward.'

Brawn, now bearded as befits a sage, and Schumacher discuss strategy as the championship beckons in 2000. (Schlegelmilch)

chapter seven

Endgame (2000)

In the close season he spent time with his family, spent four days in the Alps skiing with Ferrari – the team's traditional winter break – and, in January, two days driving the 1999 car at Barcelona. Originally he said he'd only test the new car but when the team rang and said they'd made significant modifications to the old one he changed his mind. On 17 January he covered 48 laps, and next day 66 laps. Then he flew to the warmth of Dubai with his family and spent five hours a day there training.

The new car, designated F1-2000, was unveiled in February, new partner Barrichello and Schumacher drawing the blood-red sheet back so the world could feast upon it. Todt stood nearby, small and neat and proprietorial.

We have been here before and here it all was again, the mixing of mythology and hope, the visible quickening towards another chance to tame the Horse – but this time underlaid by a question: was it the last chance? Could the team survive another miss, however near? Could Schumacher's willpower and motivation tolerate it? He seemed to give an answer soon enough when he said he intended to race until 2004, although his present contract expired at the end of 2002. He felt he wouldn't be old enough to retire then and could 'well imagine' continuing with

Ferrari for the two additional years.

The 2000 season is described here race by race. I've also given glimpses of what happened on the Fridays as well as qualifying because, although slightly repetitive, it establishes the rhythm and method which Ferrari – and Schumacher – brought to each of the race weekends. If it was essentially the same rhythm and method from Melbourne in March to the Far East in late autumn, well, that's the way it was.

Schumacher drove the F1-2000 at Fiorano on 9 February but, one way and another, didn't get into it until five minutes past six in the evening. Ferrari reported (almost whimsically) that he covered four laps but 'the time set is meaningless given that it was lapping in darkness'.

Schumacher, however, emphasised how important these laps were, even if – perhaps – that importance might be seen as symbolic. They launched the long journey and 'there were no problems with the car. The only thing that bothered me was the buffeting of the wind on my helmet. I'd like to have pushed harder but it was impossible because of the darkness.' Much later he'd add something important. 'The first time I sat in the car I knew I would be able to fight for the Championship right from the start.'

Next day he covered six laps but complained of a pain in his neck. He had a chill. 'It's a shame because I felt really comfortable in the car. Anyway, I am very optimistic because of the good lap time set.' That was 1m 01.26s, and while any such comparisons are intrinsically misleading, test driver Luca Badoer had spent three days at Fiorano in early January in the 1998 car and gone no faster than 1:02.637s; later that month, in the 1999 car, he'd got down to 1:00.226s; here, when Schumacher had departed, Badoer would get the F1-2000 down to 1:00.310s.

Schumacher tested at Mugello, then Fiorano again (1:01.991s, next day 1:01.188s), then Mugello again, then Fiorano again and flew to **Australia** feeling optimistic. 'Our optimism after getting the wind-tunnel results has been proved on the track. For the first time in many years I have a car capable of winning right from the first race. It is better than last year's car in every respect. We are even ahead of our schedule because the car is working so reliably. There was not one serious technical problem with the car during winter testing. It was almost a little bit scary how reliably the car ran all the time. When we finally had an electrical failure in Mugello I felt relieved. The car behaves like a marvel, it reacts quickly to changes in the set-up, runs reliably and is bloody fast.'

At Melbourne, Schumacher went quickest on the Friday and crashed. 'The car just got away from me and I lost control. Unfortunately there was nowhere for me to go. I am fine.' Next day in qualifying he went off onto the grass and confessed it was his own fault. He qualified third but wasn't concerned by that as he surveyed a 'long hard race'.

The McLarens led but both retired and Schumacher stroked the Ferrari home to win. 'I could match the pace at the front and I decided to take it easy and push before the pit stops. I was disappointed when the McLarens retired because I would have preferred to race them to the end to show what we could do.' He said he was looking forward to the rest of the season.

Schumacher's disappointment was understandable – Coulthard had suffered an engine problem on lap 12, Hakkinen an engine problem on lap 19 – because the theme of the season was clearly going to be whether the Ferraris could match the McLarens. The Championship would turn on that. Schumacher repeated that he'd been able to run at the McLarens' pace 'without pushing' but Ron Dennis countered that the McLarens were controlling the race before they retired.

Judgement was suspended until **Brazil** and qualifying there hardly helped because, although Schumacher qualified behind the McLarens again, he was happy enough. 'Just as in Australia, looking at my sector times shows it could have been very close. On my second run I went off the track and damaged the car's chassis over the kerb.'

From the lights Hakkinen led but Schumacher muscled past Coulthard to be second. He pressured Hakkinen: proper, old-fashioned motor racing pressure, keeping tight onto the rear of the McLaren and constantly ducking out trying to create a chance. Crossing the line to complete the opening lap he slipstreamed, jinked inside and was through. 'I did not want to take a risk too soon and of course Mika was not keen to let me past. I enjoyed our battle. It has been a long time since there has been a good fight and overtaking for the lead.'

From there he moved to victory over Coulthard (who was subsequently disqualified for a front wing infringement) although it must be said that Hakkinen, on a one-stop strategy, led again – Schumacher was on two stops. Anyway, Hakkinen's engine failed again. Schumacher won despite problems: 'On my second stint a tyre moved round on the rim and that gave me some vibration problems which upset the car's handling. We were prepared to stay out for a long second stint but we changed the strategy. Towards the end the team was not sure if

A study of a man at the absolute limit. (Schlegelmilch)

I had a problem' – an oil surge in the left-hand corners – 'so they told me to take it easy and I drove very slowly through some corners, but I could have responded if I had needed to.'

Judgement remained suspended: the McLarens had not yet run a full race distance with their cars working properly.

At **Imola** he was quick on the Friday and second to Hakkinen in qualifying next day. 'I am very upset with myself because I made a bad mistake at Rivazza on my third run. Up to that point it had been a very exciting lap and I was four-tenths up. I could easily have been on pole and I wanted to do it for all the *tifosi* and all the team who have worked so hard this weekend. All the same, I take some pleasure from being on the front row.'

I have been around long enough to know the game is not over yet

Hakkinen led but hit something on the track which damaged the belly of the McLaren to the point where it didn't feel right again and, although he kept the lead to lap 43, he'd suffered an engine cut-out. As Hakkinen pitted, Schumacher had four laps before his own stop to gain enough time for the lead after the stop. We have been here many times before. He sensed that the decisive moment of the race had come and pushed – hard.

'I had a worrying moment when I tried to lap Diniz [in the Sauber]. He tried to be nice and let me pass but it was the wrong place [the right-right of *Acque Minerale*] and I very nearly hit him. Apart from that, the race was good fun.' Indeed, yes: Schumacher 30 points, Barrichello 9, Fisichella 8, Hakkinen 6 … Coulthard 4. Some people spoke as if the Championship was already decided, perhaps because they yearned for it so much but, these April days, all such intoxicating talk was foolish. Judgement remained suspended until the McLarens had gone the distance at full bore.

Schumacher was pragmatic, circumspect and cautious. 'I have been around long enough to know the game is not over. I have seen it happen the other way around so I am prepared. The game is over when I have mathematically won the Championship.'

The **British** Grand Prix had been brought forward to April and, in the traditional testing there beforehand, Schumacher was quickest on the two days he drove. He had to deal with whatever emotions might confront him when memories of his accident came back but, as he pointed out, these 'had less of an effect on me than the accident to Zonta today'. Ricardo Zonta's BAR somersaulted at 190mph.

For Friday practice the weather was murky and miserable and Schumacher finished twenty-first. 'In these conditions it is almost impossible to drive and it is also dangerous. I would suggest to the FIA that when the weather is like this the Safety Car should be used in practice as well as the race. I had a problem with aquaplaning and it was impossible to see what was going on in front or just the distance to other cars ahead. The big problem here is that the rain does not drain away quickly enough.' Worse, the rhythm of the weekend had been disturbed: any attempt to set the car up properly proved 'almost useless'.

Next day, amidst more murk and misery, Barrichello took his first pole for Ferrari, Schumacher fifth. 'On my last run we changed the set-up but it didn't pay off. On top of that I made a couple of mistakes which cost me precious time. I am not satisfied with my grid position. However it is very important for me that my main rival for the Championship [Hakkinen] is right in front of me because my main objective is to pass him. It is impossible to predict what will happen in the race. This weather means that everything can change in a matter of minutes.'

As the red lights flicked off he became engulfed and had both left wheels fractionally on the grass. 'I had a good start but there were cars everywhere around me. I considered going up the grass …'

Schumacher, running seventh, found brother Ralf in the Williams behind him, hustling. 'I had a good fight with Ralf for the first two corners, which I enjoyed.' At Vale, Ralf outbraked him.

The clarity of greatness: he is my brother, obviously I don't want to crash into him so I cede the corner but my chance will come later to repass him.

Schumacher ran eighth and 'spent much of the race there. I was wondering if I was fighting for nothing, but if you don't give up then you can get somewhere. I was stuck behind Villeneuve [in the BAR] because, with roughly the same amount of fuel and him having good speed, it was impossible to pass.' Barrichello led, Schumacher almost 22 seconds away – and still behind Villeneuve – by lap 21. The pit stops broke up this structure and Schumacher worked his way up to third by the end. 'Thanks to a good car I was able to catch the others,' he'd say, adding that he felt happy about being third. Barrichello was halted by falling hydraulic pressure and Coulthard won from Hakkinen.

Schumacher 34, Coulthard 14, Hakkinen 12, Barrichello 9.

In **Spain** Schumacher went quickest on the Friday, concentrating on what he described as 'fine-tuning'. Because Barcelona is used so often for testing he added, with disarming candour, that it wasn't as exciting as 'when you come to a track where you have not tested'. He took pole next day, his first of the season. 'At the start I decided to do a run with two quick laps but after that I switched to doing just one. The increase in wind and temperature made it a bit more difficult towards the end. I was not happy with the car, even though I had a clean run, so we made some adjustments but they didn't work out the way I wanted.'

He finished the race fifth. At least that is what the dispassionate statistical records will always say. What really happened was typical Schumacher tumult. He led from pole, made his first pit stop and 'the lollipop man lifted it' – Schumacher reacting with the speed of a gunfighter to that – 'and then put it down. But it is impossible to stop that quickly. I felt I had driven over something and I looked in my mirror and

The Ferrari pit at Suzuka and the Italian mechanics spontaneously dedicated their hair to Schumacher's Championship. Why? Well, they are Italian. (Schlegelmilch)

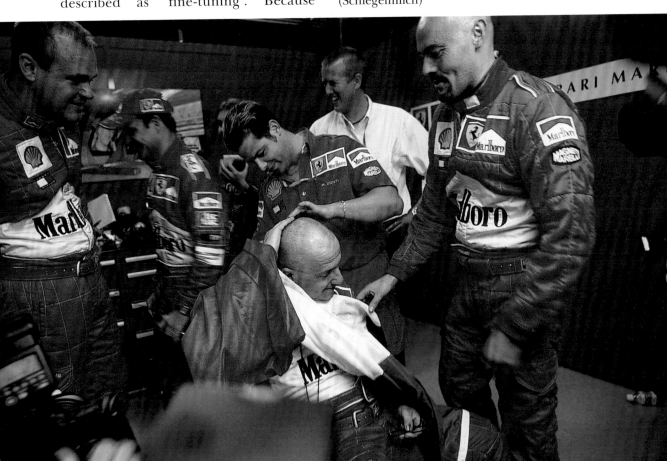

saw a mechanic on the ground [it was Stepney, the man with the refuelling nozzle, who hadn't had time to get clear of the car]. I asked the team what had happened but they didn't reply.' Stepney was taken to the track's hospital with a leg injury and a deputy was needed for Schumacher's second stop. Understandably the second stop wasn't as smooth and incisive as it would have been with Stepney and that cost precious seconds. Then Schumacher had a slow puncture 'and it was obvious the race was out of our hands'. Then he had a lively exchange with Coulthard, who was trying to overtake him.

He ruled the race and had one of the best days of his life

Schumacher blocked that 'brutally,' as one report insisted, and Coulthard said the move was unfair. Then Schumacher had a very lively exchange, spread across two or three corners, with his brother: 'As for the move with my bother, all I can say is that racing is racing.' Ralf evidently explained his feelings afterwards in blunt language and they did not leave the circuit together.

Schumacher 36, Hakkinen (who won) 22, Coulthard 20, Barrichello 13.

In the **European** Grand Prix at the Nürburgring he said 'today was a usual Friday at the office, apart from the fact that the changeable weather conditions meant we did not get as much work done as usual'. Next day he put the Ferrari on the front row (Coulthard pole). 'I am not disappointed with second place. I am sure I could have gone quicker, especially as I made a mistake at Turn 5 on my quick run – the same mistake also happened on my very last lap.' He locked brakes and the right-front tyre churned smoke. The car drifted towards the rim of the track before he brought it back.

Hakkinen made an extraordinary start to the race, slicing between Schumacher and Coulthard to lead, Schumacher behind him. 'As he moved sharply to the right,' Schumacher would say, 'I was surprised and there was nowhere I could have gone. We touched, his right rear to my left front. It was probably unnecessary and I think he knows that himself.' Hakkinen's lead endured for ten laps. Into the chicane, and with rain falling, Schumacher went to the inside, outbraked him and was through. 'It was nice,' he'd say, 'because we don't often have the opportunity to do it. I was a little bit concerned because we had the harder tyre and the conditions were very slippery but actually I made up ground.'

He dominated the rest of the race and enjoyed 'one of the best days of my life'. He hadn't won for Ferrari in Germany before. 'I have seen my fans standing here for three days in this bad weather and I hope this win has warmed their hearts a bit.' He was relaxed, he smiled broadly and he looked so fresh that, it seemed, he simply couldn't have just driven for an hour and 42 minutes in the wet at an average of some 179kmh. A reporter said he seemed to be popular here. Without a trace of irony he said 'it looks like it'. The smile broadened and he added, with a touch of irony now, 'I'm honestly not surprised I'm popular here ...'

He had judged that 'the only critical point was when it started to rain. None of us in front [Schumacher, Hakkinen, Barrichello, Coulthard] wanted to pit because it was not clear if this rain was for real. As soon as we saw others going faster on rain tyres I came in immediately. I had some problems with aquaplaning, especially towards the end, but by then I had done over 30 laps on the same tyres. In the past I have dreamed of going to Monaco with this sort of lead ...'

Schumacher 46, Hakkinen 28, Coulthard 24, Barrichello 16.

Uncharacteristically he'd preview **Monaco** by suggesting he was going there as favourite. Coulthard went quickest on the Thursday, Schumacher next. 'The car seems quite good. We have a special aerodynamic package which has given us more downforce and there are also some items specifically for this track. Tomorrow I will probably go to Fiorano to shake down our fourth car.' The Monaco meeting, of course, begins on the Thursday and continues on the Saturday: Friday is laced with the champagne of corporate hospitality. That Friday he did journey to Fiorano and covered 42 kilometres shaking-down Barrichello's spare for the Monaco race. Next day, back at Monaco, he took pole after an 'almost perfect session except that I had some understeer'. Perfection? He'd brushed the barriers a couple of times. 'I thought they needed repainting!'

He made a crisp, clean start to the race and constructed a safe lead over Trulli, who'd put his Jordan on the front row.

Hakkinen ran fifth behind Frentzen. When Trulli dropped out (gearbox) Schumacher led Coulthard by 33.657 seconds although the Scot was running fractionally quicker.

	Schumacher	Coulthard	Gain/Loss
Lap 41	1: 22.730	1: 22.271	– 0.459
Lap 42	1: 22.287	1: 22.104	– 0.183
Lap 43	1: 22.262	1: 22.309	+ 0.047

Schumacher pitted on lap 49 and emerged still in the lead but sensed he was in trouble. 'I had a problem with an exhaust pipe which damaged the left-rear suspension. I felt a few laps before that something was wrong but there was nothing I could do

about it.' The Ferrari suddenly weaved as it passed the pit lane wall but he caught that: its right front tyre was up off the ground like a broken paw. 'Obviously I am disappointed but not too much. It's true I could have picked up ten points but the driver I consider my main rival could too'. Hakkinen finished sixth. Looking sombre, Schumacher was asked about Ralf, who'd hit the barrier. 'Apparently he has quite a deep cut in his leg but nothing more than that. He had to have stitches but nothing is broken and there are no further problems. Quite lucky.'

Schumacher 46, Coulthard 34, Hakkinen 29, Barrichello 22.

He was second fastest on the Friday in **Canada** to Coulthard, making him optimistic. He translated that optimism into pole after a 'very exciting session with me being fastest, then losing it [to Coulthard] and getting it back again.'

He led throughout the race except for the necessary interregnum of pit stops and, as it happened, Coulthard was removed from any form of contention by

The microcosm of 2000 and its natural order: Schumacher, then Barrichello. (Schlegelmilch)

a 10 second stop/go penalty for an infringement on the starting grid. 'At the start I knew something had happened to Coulthard but I just drove my own race,' Schumacher said. 'He was not close enough to attack anyway then, when he had his penalty, I took it easy. I made my pit stop early because we thought something was wrong with the car but the mechanics couldn't find anything so I continued. The track was very slippery when it started to rain, then it got better and then worse. I locked my brakes at Turn 1 and decided to drive through the gravel. I am not thinking about the Championship. There's still a long way to go.' He paid tribute to Barrichello for helping with the victory – Barrichello finished an eye-blink behind him (0.174 of a second) – and said the kindness would be repaid.

Schumacher 56, Coulthard 34, Hakkinen 32, Barrichello 28.

In **France** he spent the Friday 'checking out some question marks we had left over' from the previous week's testing at the cir-

Hakkinen v Schumacher, the only duel across Schumacher's era which avoided the corrosion of human conduct. (Schlegelmilch)

cuit. He took pole. 'My first run was spot on and that is the main reason I took pole, because others seemed to improve on their later runs.'

Schumacher led Barrichello after a muscular start to the race which Coulthard didn't like and to which Schumacher would riposte: 'If he doesn't like it, he can go somewhere else.' Ron Dennis added a riposte of his own to Schumacher: 'Just because you drive a red car and have got a certain helmet design doesn't mean to say the sea is going to open in front of you every time you expect it to …'

Whatever, the McLarens were circling behind the Ferraris and completing lap 11

Barrichello	@ 5.047s
Coulthard	@ 5.975s
Hakkinen	@ 7.905s

Just before the pit stops Coulthard got past Barrichello but after them Schumacher led again although 'the tyres on my car seemed to suffer a drop in performance earlier than on the others. This problem was at its worst after the first pit stop. At first I could control the situation but then the tyres went off and I tried to look after

them because I knew there were a lot of laps to go. Then I started to slow and Coulthard got past me. Finally on lap 59 I had an engine problem and had to stop.'

In **Austria** 'we did the usual Friday job of preparing ourselves for the job. I used three sets of new tyres – because I felt like it!' Qualifying was difficult. 'On my last run I had nothing to lose. I was fourth and gave it my all but I went over the limit at Turn 4 and lost control of the car. I am quite a way off pole time [Schumacher 1:11.046, Hakkinen 1:10.410] which worries me a little. Unlike our rivals I have been unable to find the right balance between the slow and quick corners, and that is very important here. I seem to lose out to the others in the first and third sections and I was only really competitive in the second one. I could have been a bit quicker but not quick enough for the front row. I hope to make up a few places at the start …'

In the background Jacques Villeneuve was critical of Schumacher's tactics in what, after France, was being described as the Great Grand Prix Start Controversy – Schumacher swerving across the track to defend his position. Villeneuve was quoted as saying 'it does bother me. It is always the same person doing it. But why should he stop? He always gets away with it.' Evidently the subject was raised at the drivers' briefing but race director Charlie Whiting said he had no problem with what Schumacher had done at Magny Cours. Coulthard, it seems, had asked Whiting for a ruling.

The irony of that consumed Schumacher's race. 'I was going into the first corner and Zonta hit me, sending me into a spin. It's as simple as that.'

Zonta's BAR was directly behind Schumacher on the grid. The first corner, a 90 degree right, is a long way from the starting line and that allows a great deal of jostling for position. Schumacher went inside Barrichello and Zonta behind. Turning in, Zonta tapped the rear of the Ferrari, spinning it completely around so that it rotated across the corner and finished on a thin strip of grass. The main body of the runners moved away and when they were gone Schumacher drove

Three wise men – Brawn, Schumacher and Todt – distil the spirit of 2000: we are real winners now. (Schlegelmilch)

the Ferrari, front wheels askew, back onto the track. That made McLaren deduce he was trying to get the race stopped – so he'd have a re-start in the spare – but the race wasn't stopped. Schumacher walked back, helmet in hand.

He stripped to a white tee-shirt and a forest of microphones were thrust towards his face. You could forgive a man who'd just been in a car crash – and is hearing in the distance Hakkinen's McLaren going round and round towards ten Championship points – for being prickly, yet Schumacher was perfectly composed. 'Of course I am very disappointed but that is motor racing. Ricardo overestimated his own abilities and underestimated his speed but I am sure there was nothing intentional about his actions. I have made mistakes in the past and I am sure he will admit it was his fault. He was given a stop/go penalty and so the FIA has already decided who was responsible. It doesn't help to lament about it. My only regret is that I was taken out by someone who isn't a direct opponent. It was absolutely unnecessary. I will have a quiet word with him next time.'

He was asked if he felt the race should have been stopped. He smiled. 'From my position, definitely ...'

Hakkinen got the ten points, Coulthard finished second and that made it Schumacher 56, Coulthard 50, Hakkinen 48, Barrichello 36.

Later Schumacher dismissed talk of a Ferrari crisis although he spoke of everyone having to work harder; but a sense of crisis returned in **Germany** where he was quick on the Friday and put the Ferrari on the front row next day (Coulthard pole). 'On my last run the second sector was very difficult because the *Ost Kurve* and the first chicane were very wet. The third chicane was slightly better at the end but the *Motodrom* [the complex] was wet in the last two corners. In these conditions you need to have confidence. I was on the limit and I was very near going off the track.' Of the

Great Grand Prix Starts Controversy he said: 'I've been turned into the bad guy, but that is not the case. We are racing in a hard and fair way. We're not happy families out for a drive and a cup of coffee.'

The race was cast into irony again with, as it seemed, another episode in the Great Controversy. From the lights Schumacher, whose grid position was on the right, moved full over to the left and presented himself in front of Fisichella who'd say: 'I was on my line and then suddenly Michael's car was right in front of my front wheel so I went into the back of him.' Schumacher pirouetted into the barrier and expressed his 'disappointment' for what happened. 'It is very hard to accept something like this for a second race in a row.' There were consolations. Barrichello won his first race for Ferrari, which delighted Schumacher, not least because that restricted Hakkinen to second place and Coulthard to third.

Schumacher 56, Coulthard and Hakkinen 54, Barrichello 46.

During testing at Fiorano he gave an extensive interview to Derick Allsop of *The Independent*, surveying his world with that disarming candour again. 'Sure, it would be more pleasant if there were none of these polemics but the guys who are always at the front have not been there without being in this kind of situation. If I am in this situation it means I am up at the front so I honestly prefer it. Any job brings controversy. There is no job in the world without a bad side. Naturally, I sometimes feel unhappy and things could be better. I have my bad moods but nothing has gone far enough to make me want to stop, to say *that's enough.*

'I hear all these theories about jealousies and so on. I would say I have quite a lot of friends in Formula 1 but there are those I don't have a relationship with and others who don't like me in particular. But then those guys who maybe don't like me will have other drivers who don't like them. So it's nothing unusual. I have always been in a kind of spotlight. I try to look at myself and see what is true and not true. I believe what I see is not an arrogant person. I appear sometimes to people like this because I have to build up a kind of protection. I have to concentrate on my job and if that means I cannot be available to everyone then I'm sorry but it has to be this way. Most of the people understand that and don't call me arrogant.

'I'm probably too German for a lot of the *tifosi*, too serious, not enough ups and downs, not enough emotions. Not like Alesi. People love that, particularly in Italy. Plus there is the language barrier, although I have improved my Italian quite a bit. But, again, how many *tifosi* actually know me? They see me in the racing car and that's about it. It's not in my nature to go out to them. I'm a person who likes the quiet and the balance between business and privacy.'

In **Hungary** he had a 'pretty average Friday' then took pole. 'The car felt good but not perfect.' He finished second, to Hakkinen. 'All things considered I am happy with second place. I was just not fast enough. It was not such a bad start but I could see Mika behind me and then he came inside me. I kept it tight but he was there and in the end I had to open the door.'

Hakkinen 64, Schumacher 62, Coulthard 58, Barrichello 49.

In **Belgium** he was fifth quickest on the Friday – 'a reasonable day, uneventful' – and qualified fourth. 'I can't honestly say this was an entirely satisfying qualifying session for us. Being fourth, almost a second off the pole, is not what we expected. On my second run, which turned out to be my best, I was slowed by traffic in the second sector. Then on my third run I had to slow because of yellow flags.'

He led the race late on, Hakkinen coming at him hard. This was wonderful and alarming and, at its climactic moment, astonishing. On Lap 40 Hakkinen attacked into *Les Combes*, the right-hander at the top of the hill after *Eau Rouge*. We are talking here of perhaps 300kmh. As Hakkinen probed, Schumacher moved over. They were so close Hakkinen was initially unsure whether they had touched. Next lap, at the same place they had come upon Zonta who, from mid-track, obligingly moved over to the right to allow Schumacher through.

Schumacher alone distils the spirit of 2000: I am a winner. (Schlegelmilch)

Schumacher went left. Hakkinen – to Zonta's consternation – went into the tight little space on the right which gave him the racing line into *Les Combes*. It settled the race. 'I was happy to see the backmarker in front of me because I felt Hakkinen had more straightline speed and I thought it would help, but it was not enough,' Schumacher said. 'As for the passing move, usually there is only room for two cars on the track but Mika made an outstanding move. If he had not passed me there he would have done later. We do not feel we have lost the Championship.'

Hakkinen 74, Schumacher 68, Coulthard 61, Barrichello 49.

In **Italy** Barrichello was quickest on the Friday, Schumacher next. 'The car is going very well, better than in the past when we came here.' He took pole, Barrichello next. 'I messed up my first lap, running wide at the first chicane, but the car felt quick which is why I decided to go for a second lap, even if it was a bit of a risk.'

Schumacher led into the 'new' reshaped first chicane from Hakkinen, but a vast crash engulfed the midfield runners at the second chicane and a piece of debris killed a marshal, Paolo Gislimberti. When the Safety Car withdrew, Schumacher led Hakkinen again although there was a bizarre moment when, the Safety Car still out, Schumacher accelerated and the cars behind assumed he'd set off into the re-start. They accelerated too, but in fact Schumacher was warming his brakes: he braked hard to do that, causing consternation behind. Rookie Jenson Button in the Williams swerved off to avoid a collision. 'Some drivers at the back might have been caught out by this and I apologise if I caused them a problem.' Schumacher now led every lap of the race except three during the pit stops and beat Hakkinen by almost four seconds. 'At the end I backed off to be careful with the engine. I am very sad to hear about the death of a track official. Under these circumstances what happened in the race has only secondary importance.'

At the Press Conference Schumacher, who had now equalled Senna's 41 wins and lifted many burdens from himself in the Championship, suddenly broke down in convulsive tears. 'Everybody has a limit, and that was over my limit today.'

Hakkinen 80, Schumacher 78, Coulthard 61, Barrichello 49.

And they went to Indianapolis for the **United States** Grand Prix, an intriguing adaptation of the old Brickyard oval embracing a more familiar (to the Grand Prix driver) 'technical' infield. Before he journeyed to Indianapolis Schumacher confessed he'd considered retiring from the sport after the death at Monza. 'I think you always do at extreme moments like this.' Meanwhile, in the background and on another level, there were suggestions that Coulthard would now be helping Hakkinen, his own Championship hopes having all but vanished.

No Grand Prix had been run in the United States since 1991, and I cannot resist quoting from a reporter called Sandra McKee who filed this to *The Baltimore Sun*: 'In a sports-crazy country like the United States, isn't it odd that the world's highest-paid and most popular athlete is almost unknown? Isn't it odd that Michael Schumacher of Germany will be making his first professional appearance of his 10-year career here this week? Michael Who? Around the world, 31-year-old Michael Schumacher is bigger than Tiger Woods, Michael Jordan or Pete Sampras.'

She also wrote: 'Schumacher is an avid soccer player, a doting father of daughter Gina Maria, 3, and son Mick, 1, and an animal lover. Earlier this year in Brazil, Schumacher and his wife Corinna adopted a mongrel pup when it wandered into their lives, named it 'Floh' (German for 'flea') and flew it to Europe in a first-class seat.' Whether the anecdote is true I know not (nor care) and I include it only because it was obviously the sort of detail

Schumacher takes the United States Grand Prix at Indianapolis and at this instant Formula 1 went truly global again. (Schlegelmilch)

Ms McKee thought the readers in Baltimore would find interesting.

In practice and qualifying the teams discovered that along the straight you could get a 'tow' from your team-mate. Schumacher described this as 'playing team tactics'. He didn't have difficulty adapting to the circuit. 'Going round the turns on the oval is not as exciting as it might look from outside because the entry speed is not so high. There the element of danger is reduced compared to what we might have expected. The fact that the track is so flat means that it takes a few laps to find the right turn-in point for the corners.' He took pole (Coulthard next, then Hakkinen and Barrichello) and 'I was surprised at the great reception from the spectators who were cheering us on.'

Coulthard jumped the start and led on a damp track, Schumacher tucked in behind him. 'After the start we knew that Coulthard might have a [stop/go] penalty but I had to pass him because he was slowing me. Of course that was done so Mika could catch me, which is fair enough – they are team-mates.' Schumacher got a tow, made a power play but Coulthard resisted. Schumacher muscled through. 'I think he [Coulthard] tried a bit too hard to stop me and we touched.' Schumacher now concentrated on conserving his tyres while Coulthard let Hakkinen through. Hakkinen pitted for dry tyres but Schumacher stayed out ten laps longer before pitting for his.

All this became academic after 25 laps when flames licked out from Hakkinen's engine and he retired. 'I was in front when Mika went out and I believe I could have stayed there if he had continued,' Schumacher said. 'We beat them fair and square.' Mind you, Schumacher did spin on lap 69 (of the 73). 'I wasn't concentrating because I was cruising after the team told me to slow down. I got caught out on some wet grass which spun me round. Ross Brawn told me on the radio to concentrate and I replied that I was awake now ...'

Schumacher 88, Hakkinen 80, Coulthard 63, Barrichello 55.

We have come full circle. He went to **Japan** and rode the earthquake, rode out one of the tightest qualifying hours ever seen, rode out the unfolding uncertainties of the Grand Prix: trapped behind Hakkinen for what seemed an eternity, then – in a handful of moments which distilled the essence of Michael Schumacher and the essence of what, with him, Ferrari had become – he *created* the victory which echoed round the world. After the five years at Ferrari, the 74 races there, the 21 poles and 24 victories, the circle was finally completed:

Schumacher 98, Hakkinen 86, Coulthard 67, Barrichello 58.

He'd tamed the Horse.

And he rounded that off nicely in **Malaysia,** taking pole (by half a second) from Hakkinen and then holding Coulthard at bay across long tracts of the race to win it comfortably enough. Moreover, Coulthard sought him out and apologised over using the Media as a weapon in their feuding since the French Grand Prix. 'It was a very nice gesture, and I appreciate very much that he thinks like that,' Schumacher said. 'But it wasn't only him who acted in this way, because I am guilty of doing it as well. Hopefully from now on we can have a good relationship.'

It was a time for sentiments like that. Season's end often is. The future – the defence of the title – might not be so peaceful.

Schumacher had a more immediate engagement, however. Three weeks after Malaysia he went in to La Pitie Salpetiere hospital in Paris for a minor operation to remove a 30cm long pin from his right leg. It had been inserted after his crash at Silverstone in 1999. He stayed overnight and returned home to Switzerland. 'I feel fine. I am confident I will soon be mobile again with no problems and I will continue to enjoy my holidays. That way, I'll be in top form when it's time to start work again.'

Testing resumed at Fiorano on 4 December, with Luca Badoer driving. Ferrari said that, after the November break, they were testing 'new components and electronics'.

The future had begun.

Michael Schumacher: career statistics

Abbreviations:
P – pole; FL – fastest lap: DNF – did not finish

Up to 1996

Karting

1984 and 1985 German Junior Champion;
1985 Junior World Championship, 2;
1986 European Championship, 3;
1987 German Senior Champion and European Champion.

Car racing

1988 Formula Koenig Champion;
1989 German Formula 3, joint second;
1990 German Formula 3 Champion;
1991 Sportscar World Championship (Mercedes), joint 9th.

Grand Prix racing

Debut 1991 Spa (Jordan);
then Benetton up to signing for Ferrari – 69 races, 10 pole positions, 19 wins, World Champion 1994 and 1995.

1996

Ferrari F310

Date	Race	Result
10 Mar	Australia, Melbourne	DNF
31 Mar	Brazil, Sao Paulo	3
7 Apr	Argentina, B Aires	DNF
28 Apr	Europe, Nürburgring	2
5 May	San Marino, Imola	P/2
19 May	Monaco, Monte Carlo	P/DNF
2 Jun	Spain, Barcelona	FL/1
16 Jun	Canada, Montreal	DNF
30 Jun	France, Magny-Cours	P/DNF
14 Jul	Britain, Silverstone	DNF
28 Jul	Germany, Hockenheim	4
11 Aug	Hungary, Hungaroring	P/9
25 Aug	Belgium, Spa	1
8 Sep	Italy, Monza	FL/1
22 Sep	Portugal, Estoril	3
13 Oct	Japan, Suzuka	2

D. Hill 97, J. Villeneuve 78, Schumacher 59.

1997

Ferrari F310B

Date	Race	Result
9 Mar	Australia, Melbourne	2
30 Mar	Brazil, Sao Paulo	5
13 Apr	Argentina, B Aires	DNF
27 Apr	San Marino, Imola	2
11 May	Monaco, Monte Carlo	FL/1
25 May	Spain, Barcelona	4
15 Jun	Canada, Montreal	P/1
29 Jun	France, Magny-Cours	P/FL/1
13 Jul	Britain, Silverstone	FL/DNF
27 Jul	Germany, Hockenheim	2
10 Aug	Hungary, Hungaroring	P/4
24 Aug	Belgium, Spa	1
7 Sep	Italy, Monza	6
21 Sep	Austria A1 Ring	6
28 Sep	Luxembourg, Nürburgring	DNF
12 Oct	Japan, Suzuka	1
26 Oct	Europe, Jerez	DNF

Villeneuve 81, Schumacher 78, Frentzen 42.*
*(*Because of the Jerez incident with Villeneuve, Schumacher was excluded from the final classification.)*

1998

Ferrari F300

Date	Race	Result
8 Mar	Australia, Melbourne	DNF
29 Mar	Brazil, Sao Paulo	3
12 Apr	Argentina, B Aires	1
26 Apr	San Marino, Imola	FL/2
10 May	Spain, Barcelona	3
24 May	Monaco, Monte Carlo	10
7 Jun	Canada, Montreal	FL/1
28 Jun	France, Magny-Cours	1
12 Jul	Britain, Silverstone	FL/1
26 Jul	Austria, A1 Ring	3
2 Aug	Germany, Hockenheim	5
16 Aug	Hungary, Hungaroring	FL/1
30 Aug	Belgium, Spa	FL/DNF
13 Sept	Italy, Monza	P/1
27 Sep	Europe, Nürburgring	P/2
1 Nov	Japan, Suzuka	P/FL/DNF

Hakkinen 100, Schumacher 86, Coulthard 56.

1999
Ferrari F399

Date	Race	Result
7 Mar	Australia, Melbourne	FL/8
11 Apr	Brazil, Sao Paulo	2
2 May	San Marino, Imola	FL/1
16 May	Monaco, Monte Carlo	1
30 May	Spain, Barcelona	FL/3
13 Jun	Canada, Montreal	P/DNF
27 Jun	France, Magny-Cours	5
11 Jul	Britain, Silverstone	DNF
25 Jul	Austria, A1-Ring	Absent
1 Aug	Germany, Hockenheim	Absent
15 Aug	Hungary, Hungaroring	Absent
29 Aug	Belgium, Spa	Absent
12 Sept	Italy, Monza	Absent
26 Sept	Europe, Nürburgring	Absent
17 Oct	Malaysia, Kuala Lumpur	P/FL/2
31 Oct	Japan, Suzuka	P/FL/2

Hakkinen 76, Irvine 74, Frentzen 54 (Schumacher fifth, 44).

2000
Ferrari F1-2000

Date	Race	Result
12 Mar	Australia, Melbourne	1
26 Mar	Brazil, Sao Paulo	FL/1
9 Apr	San Marino, Imola	1
23 Apr	Britain, Silverstone	3
7 May	Spain, Barcelona	P/5
21 May	Europe, Nürburgring	FL/1
4 Jun	Monaco, Monte Carlo	P/R
18 June	Canada, Montreal	P/1
2 Jul	France, Magny-Cours	P/R
16 Jul	Austria, A1 Ring	R
30 Jul	Germany, Hockenheim	R
13 Aug	Hungary, Hungaroring	P/2
27 Aug	Belgium, Spa	2
10 Sep	Italy, Monza	P/1
24 Sep	USA, Indianapolis	P/1
8 Oct	Japan, Suzuka	P/1
22 Oct	Malaysia, Kuala Lumpur	P/1

Schumacher 108, Hakkinen 89, Coulthard 73.

Career record
Michael Schumacher's career record in Grand Prix racing, at 1 January 2001: 145 races, 3 World Championships, 32 pole positions, 41 fastest laps, 44 wins, 678 points

Monaco, 2000. (Schlegelmilch)

Index